Praise for *Leap With M*

"*Leap With Me* contains the truth about our creativity. Laurie shares her struggle and even mystical feelings about when and how this book was born. I know the truth and it is that we all have guides and angels who are here to teach us the way. When you let your thinking and intellect open to your consciousness and feelings, magic happens. So read on and be guided to your true self and know that when you leap, someone is holding your hand."
~Bernie Siegel, MD, *New York Times* and International Bestselling Author of 19 books including *When You Realize How Perfect Everything Is, No Endings Only Beginnings,* and *Love, Medicine & Miracles*

Leap With Me is a book I've been longing for. Reading it is as if Laurie's soul is speaking to mine. I can see using it with my clients, especially with teens as they often feel (and get!) so much pressure to decide what they 'want to do' with their lives. *Leap With Me* can be a wonderful tool for them to learn the steps that come before discovering our life passion and calling, namely finding our FLOW! This book is beautiful, one the world needs to experience."
~Noreen O'Sullivan, Educator and Author of *Look, Listen, Love: A Parent and Child's Guide to Emotional Freedom Tapping*

"Laurie understands how our creative energy lives within us and the ways in which we can steadily coax it out from where it hides and shape it into manifested forms. Laurie keeps a steady gaze on her own innate creativity and soul and from this natural inclination towards her own process, she skillfully supports others with compassion, wisdom and an array of effective tools."
~Donna Sherman, MSW, Creator of *Yoga Nidra with Donna Sherman: Total Relaxation Practices for Adults & Teens* and Host of the *Sparks In Action Podcast: Uplifting Each Other One Action at a Time*

"*Leap With Me* is a total delight to read and to experience! It is a fun and loving gift to all of us—those who consider themselves creative and those who don't—to take that next step into the river of flow where magic happens, and life unfolds with grace and awe!

Laurie writes: *"weaving our golden threads doesn't have to be a lonely pursuit"* and she has illustrated this so perfectly - just enough to crack open the safe space to be vulnerable in sharing that which is yet unformed from the quiet place inside as it takes shape and becomes infused with a life all its own. I highly recommend this book—it's a perfect companion for your journey into flow."
~Maureen Theresa Smith, Creator of Indigo Blooms and Indigo Circles, Intuition Medicine® Practitioner and Author of *Your Moontime Magic: A Girl's Guide to Getting Your Period and Loving Your Body* and *Your First Moon: Celebration and Support for a Girl's Growing Up Journey*

"Laurie Smith in her beautiful and soulful book, *Leap with Me,* guides readers on a journey of self-reflection and provides tools for getting unstuck. She tells us, *"A leap is a positive step we take to honor, nurture, or share our True Self in a new way. When we leap, the energy of our True Self shines."* Laurie gently challenges readers to embrace their true creative self with a wide array of prompts, like journaling, art/singing exercises, and meditations. Her essays are uplifting and healing in nature, and her tender poems bring productive emotions or tears to the surface. She is a gifted essayist, who invites readers to tap into intuition to find or rediscover joy in life.

I have followed Laurie Smith's writings and courses for two decades, watching her growth as she supports us, her readers, to grow with her. She is both a positive and inspiring author who nudges her readers and students to expand their perspectives and embrace wonderful new possibilities and outcomes."
~June Cook, Founder of SelfHealingExpressions.com, a pioneer in the world of online learning, and author of the online course *Holistic Prayers: Healing the Mind, Body & Spirit Through Prayer*

Leap With Me

Other books by Laurie E. Smith:

Soul Wisdom

Spirit In Disguise

Leap With Me

A Creative Path to
Finding and Following
Your True Voice

By Laurie E. Smith

Spreading Sunshine Books
San Francisco, CA

Published by: Spreading Sunshine Books llc
SpreadingSunshineBooks.com
San Francisco, CA

This book is for the enjoyment of the reader and designed to support readers in taking responsibility for their own well-being. The author, publisher, and this book make no claim of providing specific results or healing. This book is not meant to replace professional therapy, treatment, or support.

If you choose to use the information in this book in your own professional practice or to support your own clients or students, please provide credit, author contact information, and comply with the above copyright laws. The author can be reached at Laurie@LaurieSmith.com and www.LaurieSmith.com for reprints and special requests.

While the author has made every effort to provide accurate quotations, sources, and Internet addresses at the time of publication, neither the publisher nor the author assumes any responsibility for errors, or for changes that occur or new information that is revealed after publication. The author and publisher do not have control over and do not assume any responsibility for author or third-party websites, books or other sources for quoted material or their content.

Hummingbird image used under enhanced image license: Shutterstock.com.
Photographer: Nature and Glass

Library of Congress Control Number: 2022910698

Smith, Laurie
ISBN: 978-0-9778022-2-7

More information about Laurie's work can be found at: **www.LaurieSmith.com**

For you, my friend

This book is for you,
with gratitude.

Whether or not we have met, we are connected
through our creative callings.

May this book keep you company
when your life is happily flowing along.

And on days when it's not,
may it support you in reconnecting with
your inner voice.

You have unique gifts
no one else in the world has
or ever will.

The world needs you,
your light, and your leaps!

Hi friend!

I don't know about you, but when I'm feeling overwhelmed, sometimes, my brain momentarily freezes. Then it travels out and grasps at the first idea it can find to keep me moving forward.

That's what happened the day I started writing this book. It was the first day of the COVID-19 lockdown. I was sitting in our living room, on a big, cozy chair that usually brings me comfort.

I stared at my phone, trying to make sense of the email I had just gotten from our kids' school. School closed? As my brain went on overload, an idea flitted by, a welcome distraction. The idea wasn't earthshattering, but it changed my life.

This book is the story of what happened when I followed that idea, and what I've learned about creative flow along the way. I believe we are constantly being invited to create turnarounds in our lives. Intuitive thoughts flutter by, grabbing our attention, reminding us that we can transform outer chaos into inner beauty.

No matter what is happening *out there*, we each have a wise inner voice coaxing us to find miracles in life's messiness and inviting us on joyful, creative adventures. All we need to do is say YES.

If you are looking to strengthen your relationship with your true, inner voice, create your own turning point, or embark on your own life-changing journey, I've written this book for you.

I'm so glad you're here. I can't wait to take this journey together.

The Hummingbird

Little messenger arrives
like an unexpected
creative fragment,

wings beating like my heart.

Let us enjoy our time
while we are still

Together

she sings,
before we both
flit away

forever changed
by having met.

Contents

"The artist never entirely knows. We guess. We may be wrong, but we take leap after leap in the dark."

~Agnes de Mille

I wasn't ready for *this.*

Depending on how you look at it, this book is either a gift or an unexpected guest. It came without warning, invading my life, derailing my plans and habitual ways of living.

Yet, isn't that the way it is with most breakthroughs? By breakthrough, I literally mean something broke through—broke through my clutter, broke through my chattering mind, broke through my hopes and fears, dreams, and commitments.

This book broke through all that was happening in the foreground of my life. It made its way in sneakily at first. One little poem and word here, one there. Jotted down on envelopes, napkins, tissues, receipts, and magazine covers. Everywhere.

I wrote this book when it was inconvenient. I wrote it when I didn't want to write. I wrote it when I should have been doing more important things.

This book is like an intrusive and endearing friend who tells us an unwelcome truth, then loyally holds our hand as we slowly accept it. She barged her way into my darkest places, my messiest closets to see my clutter, dirty clothes, neglected treasures, underwear strewn on the floor, then shared it all with *you*.

Here it is. Here it *all* is. This is who she *really* is. Wow. That's scary—and liberating. I think this is how our True Self often gets through. She messily barges her way into our lives, often scaring the heck out of us. She also embarrasses us—blowing our covers, our well-manufactured personas and sense of self.

True Self breaks us out of our self-imposed facades any way she can. She clamors her way into our lives when we least expect it—during tragedy, heartbreak, depression, when we're on our way to the top, achieving and going places, when we think we know better, and when we have no time. *Especially* when we have no time.

In those rare moments in between all the busyness of our lives when we let our guard down and forget to block the dam, when we accidentally grab the torn envelope to jot down what we've heard (half wondering if we've gone mad), something leaps. Personally, I think it's our heart, leaping for joy like when a loved one returns home after being away for too long.

When we hear our inner voice, we return home. Home to our musings. Home to our imperfections. Home to our craziness and confusion. Home to inspiration. Home to our own unique rhythm. Home to something greater. Home to flow.

It is amidst those fragments that leap in and out of our lives when we are busy with more important things, like making sure everything is perfect, buttering up to try to win their approval, and trying to be who we think we are *supposed* to be, that pure gold arrives, frequently disguised as an intruder, and changes everything. At least, that's the way it felt to me.

You might not feel like this book is filled with gold. And that's okay. All I wish is that you feel like *your* breakthroughs are. I believe we all reach a moment in life when we know we need to move beyond where we are. I'm sharing this book of poems and prompts with you just in case you know what I mean about inner whispers and creative fragments showing up uninvited, or if you, like me, yearn to experience something more in your life, even if you are not yet sure what that may be.

At some point, we decide it's time do to something about our yearnings, to share and live life as who we *really* are, to accept joy, let go of struggle, and have our lives start flowing instead.

Creative leaps are not always graceful, beautiful, or turn out the way we think they will. We often feel ridiculous. Sometimes we take leaps spontaneously, completely unprepared for the changes that happen when we do. Other times we plan and debate, trying to get all our details perfect first. As soon as our feet have left the ground, we may convince ourselves we've made a mistake, simply because we are not used to how leaping feels.

That's why it can be helpful to gather with others who know the yearning to try something new, to go beyond where we've gone before—whether through letting go of an old unwanted habit, launching a creative hobby or artistic endeavor, or simply having more authentic conversations about what's really going on in our hearts and minds.

When we take intuitive and creative leaps of courage into the void, into the black holes of our own consciousness, our hearts leap out along with us. Sometimes we're lucky and when we're mid-leap, hanging out there in mid-air, we discover that we are not alone and never have been.

Life holds out her two hands to meet us and we are caught.

> *"You only live once, but if you do it right, once is enough."*
>
> *~Mae West*

Ready to Leap

Leap With Me

When It's Time for a Change

Every now and then, we reach a point in life where we know it's time for a change. It might start as feeling stuck or bored. We might feel sad about dreams that have not yet come true or frustrated that our old way of doing things isn't working anymore. Or we may simply wish that we had more time, or more control over the limited time that we do have.

When we experience feelings like this, it's natural to think they are personal, about us, who we are and the unique details of our lives. The truth is, however, we are not alone. People all over the world right now in this exact moment are having similar thoughts and feelings.

It's also easy to get lured into thinking that the answer is out there somewhere, in some magical program or guidebook, in some grand gesture or action we need to take. In my experience, the first step—often the most important leap of all—is one we take within.

The key to making a change, to getting our lives to really flow, to following our inner callings always begins with an inner commitment to honor who we really are. It's a private, solitary act. We start a conversation—a conversation with our Truest Selves.

We each have a small, still voice within that guides us, even when we are distracted by louder ones. Whether it's finding inner peace in a world that is anything but peaceful, making the most of the time we have on this earth, or launching our lives in some positive new direction, the way forward always begins with connecting with this inner voice and reclaiming our own unique brand of creativity.

Our ability to create is something we all have in common, no matter who we are. We can create beautiful or ugly things, depending on the day. We can create a story that scares us, keeping us frozen or stuck, or we can create one of hope, luring us out of our complacency to the next best thing.

The True Self is an artist. Her voice comes in the form of intuition, and her creativity is seen in the many ways she gets our attention—through symbols, metaphors, crazy ideas, and gut feelings— doing whatever she can to coax us to share our sparks, our unique gifts, and who we really are with the world.

We Are All Creative

Because much of this book focuses on creativity and the creative pathways our intuition often guides us to, it will likely resonate with you if you already do creative work or have a creative hobby. But another key part of this book is about that relationship we have with ourselves—our own inner voice, that essence that is difficult to describe and has an enormous impact on how we feel about our choices and our lives.

In its simplest form, creativity is about experiencing life in a way that others may not in any given moment, and then having the courage to share. And so, we are all creative. We each also have unique gifts, and an inner voice—the voice of the Truest Self—calling us to live life as only we can.

Learning Through Living

For more than two decades, I've been studying, coaching, and teaching workshops on intuition, creativity, and many different practices for connecting with our Truest Selves. I've learned the most, however, from my children, my role as a parent, and the ups and downs of my own life. Having an authentic, honest relationship with who we really are is not a one-time thing, something we master then move on to the next thing. It is a way of living and moving through the ever-changing world, an art I personally am continually practicing.

This book is about finding and following our own unique paths to taking creative leaps. You have an important perspective and story to tell, and unique gifts that the world really needs. My wish is that this book will support you in sharing the gift of *you* just as you are right now in this moment, as fully as you possibly can.

The 28-Day Flow Challenge

When I started writing this book, I was longing for more control over my life, which was becoming more and more unpredictable every day. It was the start of the pandemic. Perhaps you too struggled with anxiety as we all faced so much uncertainty.

In those first days of the COVID-19 lockdown, when so much of what we had taken for granted was being taken away, I got an idea. I would do something daily for 28 days that brought me joy and got me in a state of flow—that amazing zone where we are so into what we are doing that we often lose track of time.

Since I have always loved to write, the activity I first chose was writing. At first, it was difficult to carve out even a few minutes every day to commit to my own joy. On good days, I would roll out of bed, pen in hand, writing random journal entries on the pages of spiral-bound notebooks. On tough days, I would completely forget, quickly jotting down a few notes just to keep my commitment to myself before going to sleep at night.

Gradually, however, as is so often the case when we do something again and again, something shifted. I started hearing the voice—my own creative voice chatting away behind the emotions and busyness of everyday. The more I listened, the more interesting things became. My experiment became less about writing and more about paying attention. Before I knew it, I had reclaimed a regular, daily writing practice and a little piece of myself. I also started feeling much more inspired, hopeful, and empowered. My life started to flow in wonderful new ways.

When I saw how much my joyful flow activity was helping me, I started inviting friends to join in too. Each person who joined chose a different activity that brought them joy and helped them reclaim their own joy and connection with their inner voice. Some chose doodling, meditating, or walking. Others chose swinging, dancing, and sketching. Choosing our own unique activities was part of the fun.

The changes most of us experienced were small at first, mini energy shifts rather than dramatic transformations. But slowly, these little shifts began to build momentum. Over time, friends invited friends. Synchronicities and connections happened that almost seemed miraculous; a supportive, intuitive, creative community was born.

Not A Poet

In my own life, the more I listened, the more I wrote. Over time, I started feeling more like a scribe than a writer, simply taking down what I was hearing from a voice chatting away inside my mind. It was almost as if, in all those many years of not writing on a regular basis, the words had stacked up by the door, clogging things up, making me feel stuck. Now that I started to write again, the door opened and the waiting words tumbled out, relieved to be set free.

I started hearing words in between everyday tasks like taking out the garbage, taking a shower, or driving the kids to school. Instead of journal entries or essays, what I had been writing for most of my life, poems started happening instead, even though I *never* saw myself as a poet or even had a desire to write them.

I would wake up in the middle of the night with a poem on my mind and stay up until the first light of sunbreak, writing several more. Once I told my inner voice I was willing to experiment and play, it seemed like a faucet turned on, and things *really* started to flow, both in my creativity and my life. For the period of a week, poems didn't just flow, they stalked me. They seemed to follow me wherever I went—interrupting me in the middle of a meal, visiting me at night, waking me up—literally and spiritually.

In just over one week, all the poems on these pages—81 total—had been delivered and then, as quickly as they came, I was done, at least for the time being. During that week, I felt as if words were falling from the sky, and it was my job to hold out my paper to save a few before they shattered to the ground. In making space for these poems to come alive, I was reminded that it's not up to us where our inner voice is calling us to go. Instead, our job is simply to get out of the way.

When I shared a few of these poems—which focus primarily on the ups and downs of living a creative life—in my weekly email newsletter, I frequently got messages back from readers telling me how the poems struck a chord and resonated with their own personal experiences. Often these messages were from people who, like me, were simply living their lives, struggling with their own private journeys. I realized that these poems might offer comfort and support for others who were seeking to reconnect with a sense of peace, and to take more leaps—whether creative ones, or courageous acts of accepting and being true to themselves and the unique way they connect with the world.

Rather than simply sharing the poems as a collection, I decided to also create prompts to accompany the poems based on my professional experience. My wish was that these prompts would offer a springboard for others who, like me, were yearning for honest discussions about the real deal—the challenges and yearnings we often experience when we are committed to a relationship with our inner voice while also living very busy and complicated lives.

Finding Threads of Gold

Our creative journeys are different every time, and different for each of us. Typically, they are solitary ventures, private intimate adventures for one. We go deep, letting ourselves get tossed about by our inner currents until we find a still point. There, we find a thread to hold onto, one that feels important and for a reason that we may not fully understand, we hold on tight and thrash our way back out into the world again.

Sometimes the journey back outward is as tumultuous as the one in. We get tossed about. We might feel anxious and afraid. We might struggle. On the other hand, we might start to feel a new sense of peace as we hold tight to that thread that feels important—the thread of truth, of uniqueness, of what our inner voice is saying to us *today*.

But then what? We come out, clinging to that thread we've found, thinking we've found gold and that's enough, and suddenly we realize that's only the beginning. Worse yet (or better, depending on our state of mind at the time), our journey is not so private anymore.

We often emerge from our own inner wanderings with a dazed look on our face, holding this discovered thread that inside looked like pure gold and we realize that no one else understands its preciousness like we do. Either we let ourselves feel embarrassed that we thought we had found a treasure and others don't see it that way, bury it and pretend it never happened, or we accept that our job is not done. Next, we need to do something with what we've been given. If we don't, it might start to drive us mad.

When Creativity Flows

Depending on our state of mind, that yearning, that calling to do something with that golden thread of inspiration, to weave it into something that can be seen, touched, heard, and felt by others is another story altogether. How we handle that challenge becomes the story of our lives.

Sometimes we get to work right away, like the dutiful weaver following orders from some greater place. We might paint a picture, write a poem, take a photo, sculpt clay, write music, start humming a tune, or simply start living differently, weaving the insight gained from our creative journeying in a way that changes life for us and those around us. Other times, we may get busy and distracted by the outer world again, leaving inspiration to find its own way gradually and stealthily, making itself known only in the gaps between being busy with other things.

No matter how it happens, as our creative thread evolves, something new begins to be released on its own into the world. The very fact that we, as its guardians, have brought it out into the light changes our history and our own personal perceptions of what is possible for us and our lives.

When Creativity is Blocked

That's one way the story might go. There are other options, of course. We might pretend our creative threads don't exist, never existed, that we are crazy, or talk ourselves out of continuing with our creative imaginings, telling ourselves it really doesn't matter, or that *we* really don't matter. That might be easier, we may think, than facing our critics whether real, imagined, or remembered.

We might try to forget our creative callings, deny that our inner journeying went so deep, or that for a few moments, life felt so rich.

We might splinter our sense of self into two, unable to make sense of the vast difference between our inner and outer selves.

Or we may feel overwhelmed, weighed down by too much to do, not knowing where or how to begin as outer requests slow our flow or encroach on the avenue to ourselves. We might decide we have to go it alone, too inexperienced to know that there are others like us who have also touched gold and who are also trying, each in their own way, to make sense of their own inner whispers and inspirations, forgetting that weaving our golden threads doesn't have to be a lonely pursuit.

A Circle of Friends

Finding each other—deep, kindred, intuitive, creative spirits—really helps. Creative seeker finding seeker—others who know the joy and the pain, the delight, and the struggle, and who are so busy diving deep for their own threads that they have no desire to keep us from finding ours—changes lives. We are the ones cheering each other on through the ethers even if we haven't yet met. We are the ones, beckoning to each other through dark nights to keep the faith, to continue, begin, or start again. Even during the most solitary of missions, we are never alone.

That's because as we learn to trust the value of our own inner threads, we also start to understand that it's not just the threads within us that are gold, so too are those within each person on the face of the earth. We also come to know, whether we at first understand it or not, that all our threads are part of the same interconnected story.

With that realization, suddenly, the creative, intuitive path has the potential to become one of the most supportive, soul-connective experiences of being known and supported that we could have ever imagined possible. We remember our purpose, our collective purpose. Each of us is unique, equally capable of weaving, finding, and sharing gold.

When we find people who are willing to talk about their own journeys of feeling called, of navigating their messy closets of pain and potential, of discovering their own creative sparks, suddenly we realize that our creative adventure is not a journey for one, but for One. This realization can be incredibly healing, not just for each of us personally, but also for the world.

Your Turning Point

Being creative and intuitive means being open, like a wide-open invitation for everything life has to offer to have its way with us, from miracles to deep pain. Most of the time, our souls are expansive enough to hold it all. Occasionally, though, input from the outer world becomes too much, and we don't know what to do with some of it.

We may think that it is our job to fix the pain we notice "out there" instead of realizing that just the act of channeling our noticing, feeling, and dreaming into how we live our lives is enough. We might forget that the simplest motions of our lives can help us transcend suffering and give birth to beauty—sending out into the world something brand new.

We might fail to remember that, instead of holding on tight or trying to fix what is broken, we can let life be what it is and simply fold it into our imaginings. Rather than trying to hold it all, we can let life's input flow through us. We can alchemize it into something beautiful, even the pain.

This book is about all of this, which of course, happens completely uniquely for each of us. It couldn't be any other way. There are no rules on the journey of life, no guidebook, no answers that some expert is going to hand down to us if we just wait long enough. Instead, living creatively and intuitively is about allowing ourselves to be who we really are and to bring into form something that has never existed before.

We each have our own path, our own formula to follow. There is no one more qualified than *you* to figure out how to manifest your own personal turning point, a miracle in your own life.

A Path to the True Self

Creative peaks come and go like waves; they rise and fall. If we are paying attention and willing to go along for the ride without knowing where we will end up or even whether we will survive (at least the version of who we think we are), well then, creating is just the thing. The process becomes the goal—the gift that saves us regardless of where it takes us, or others' interpretations of our work and who they think we should be.

The highs and lows of a creative sojourn—tuning into and following where our True Selves are guiding us to go—are completely natural, but when they happen to us, we may struggle, doubting our inner voice or the very idea of who we are and what we have to offer.

That's why we need each other. We need communities of support, people who know our struggle even if we don't officially know each other. The more we reach out, share our insights, and offer support, the more we come to understand that we are not actually leaping alone but creating something beautiful as we all leap together.

I believe connecting with our inner voice and sharing what we hear is one of the surest paths to peace, happiness, and the healing of hearts and minds. My greatest wish is that within these pages you find support for your own journey and a fervent cheer to keep weaving your own filaments of gold into the magic of this, your one magnificent life.

The world needs your voice, your gifts, and your message. The world needs *you*.

"May the dreams you've kept safe in your heart keep leading you boldly through life. How this world has been waiting for YOU!"

~Anne Calodich Fone

How to Use this Book

Before we dive in, I thought it might be helpful to give you a quick overview of how this book is organized. This book integrates everything from the vulnerability of my own soul-searching reflected through my poems; my own personal life story through the memoir-like essays that begin each chapter; and a myriad of different coaching, energy healing, meditative, and personal growth processes I've trained in and have found to be useful in my own life and with my clients over the last few decades. My goal has been to weave all of this together as a strong springboard you can use to launch your own unique creative adventure.

The Heart of this Book

The heart of this book is in the next section – *Section Two.* There you will find seven chapters, each which focuses on a different creative touchstone. These touchstones can keep us moving forward by reminding us why we leap and offering a pathway we can follow. The seven touchstones are *Inspiration, Process, Blocks, Life, Circles, Calling,* and *Your Next Leap.*

Because this book is all about hearing and trusting our own creative, inner voice, I've designed it so that we can each plot our own course, depending on what we most need at any moment. Each touchstone begins with a personal story from my own life followed by a series of related poems, prompts and quotes.

For each prompt, I've shared some basic information, like how long it will take and what tools you will need. These are guidelines only. There is no right or wrong way to do the prompts, only what is right for *you*. In addition, while many of the prompts provide ideas for creative or writing projects, the focus is not on the quality of what you create, but rather how you *feel* as you respond to the prompts, answer the questions, and apply the insights you gain to your own life.

Designing Your Own Unique Adventure

Choosing how to work with the material within this book can be part of the fun, an intuitive exercise in its own right. You might read it from start to finish, doing all the prompts along the way. Then you may want to return to those sections or prompts that feel as if they can offer special gifts for you and your own life.

You could also set your own schedule for working with the material, going through this book as it were a course, for example taking a week to explore each of the seven creative touchstones, or doing one poem and prompt per day.

You could even embark on your own creative retreat and complete all the prompts during a long weekend or vacation getaway, or extend your retreat over multiple weekends, for example, diving into each touchstone every Saturday morning for seven weeks.

Another fun option is to randomly open this book to any page and see what speaks to you. This is one of my favorite ways to read a book. I'm often amazed by how doing this leads me to some new insight or piece of wisdom at the perfect time.

In the next chapter, we'll talk more about the strategy behind the prompts and how they can help us integrate our own wisdom and support us in taking more creative leaps. In the back of the book, in *Section Three,* I've included an index of common life challenges we all face, like relationship issues, setting boundaries, or finding a sense of life purpose, and which prompts can address each, to help you design your adventure to meet what you most need at this time in your life.

Following Joy and Passion

Our True Selves often communicate with us through joy and passion. If you find yourself getting excited about an idea or prompt, it likely has something valuable to offer you personally. It might be helpful to set aside extra time to explore what piques your curiosity or interest, or to come back and repeat those prompts again. When in doubt, listen to your body. When something is most helpful to us on our own individual journeys, our bodies often relax. We might even feel something shift, as if we've become lighter.

Honoring Resistance

Resistance can also be important intuitive direction. Sometimes we think resistance is a sign that we need to skip something. However, resistance can also represent a yearning to lovingly get to know parts of ourselves or our stories that we often avoid, but we may simply not know how to begin. Resistance can also be a reminder to go slow, seek compassion, and take some extra time to integrate a new idea. Or it could be a sign that we need to proceed with care or do other work or prompts to strengthen ourselves first, and then explore a new idea or perspective.

The key is having respect for resistance when it comes up for us, being kind to ourselves, taking breaks, and trusting our instincts about our own pace, and what is in our best interest. Not everything is right for all of us, and that's completely okay. We are all on different paths, with different experiences, and need different things at different times. Even the private conversations we have with ourselves as we find our path through this book can lead to transformation or head us in a new direction.

Space to Hear Your Own Voice

As you explore this book, you might notice that the sections with the poems and prompts have been formatted to include extra white space. Think of the spaces throughout this book as an invitation to tune into your own thoughts and feelings, integrate what you are reading, connect with your own inner voice, and to take deep breaths. You might also want to use these areas to jot down your own insights and ideas as they come to you about what is right for *you*.

Creating Your *Leap Journal*

Our relationship with the soft, still voice within is like any other—the more energy we put into it, the more gifts we receive. Something powerful happens when we move thought into action. Action helps us embody the wisdom of our True Selves much more deeply.

Taking action can be as simple as writing our ideas down with pen and paper. Throughout this book, I frequently mention something I call a *Leap Journal*. This is a centralized place where we can complete the prompts provided, jot down insights, and experiment with the creative practices.

You can choose a new spiral notebook, use a three-ring binder filled with paper, or select a special journal for this purpose, such as the *Leap Journal* I created as a companion to this book. It can be fun to find creative ways to make this journal your own, perhaps by decorating its cover or inner pages with images and words that inspire you. Your *Leap Journal* can become an important record to look back on later in your journey, and to help you integrate your own personal insights along the way.

Invite a Creative Friend

It can be helpful to travel through the pages of this book a friend. You could partner with a buddy and go through this process together, find a coach or therapist to support you, or join a group or tap the additional resources offered through my website LaurieSmith.com. It's amazing the synchronicities that can happen when we embark on a journey with open hearts, with supportive friends by our side, ready for adventure. Even our creative inner voices can become like loving companions, supporting us in taking leaps.

Trust Your Own Process

This book is a roadmap you can follow to design your own personal creative adventure. The most important thing is to trust what works for *you*. Be flexible and creative in the way you journey through this book. You are the expert when it comes to your own life, and the leaps your True Self is calling you to take. As you find your own path, trust your intuition. Honor what is in *your* best interest and where your intuitive, creative voice is guiding you to go.

> *"All good things have small beginnings. The mighty oak starts from a tiny acorn. From a tiny seed the most wonderful plants and flowers spring forth. From a tiny seed of love many lives can be changed."*
>
> ~Eileen Caddy

The Magic of Integration

There is no right or wrong way to get our lives to flow, to be creative, or to do the prompts in this book. I say this often because I believe it's something we all need to hear—I know I do. Most of us have been raised to live our lives focused on seeking approval from some outer influence, like a parent, teacher, or peers, rather than to trust and connect with our True Self, our own soft, still voice within.

The more we soften and become flexible and open to the idea that there may be more going on than we could ever fathom, the more miraculous shifts and changes often start to occur. I don't know about you, but my ability to hear the voice of my True Self changes depending on my own emotional state as well as what's coming at me from the outside. That's what makes the process of finding and following our creative inner voice such an adventure. Integrating our own wisdom and all of who we really are is an ongoing process rather than a onetime event.

We can think of the process of integration like weaving a braid. The braid is the core of who we are, our sense of self and how we have made peace with what has happened to us in our lives. Every once in a while, there are those stragglers, those pieces of yarn and thread that get away from us and end up sticking out at random spots, distracting and diffusing our energy. These might be anything from memories that still bug us, or the inner critics that sometimes get in our way. The more we can integrate those stragglers back into the core of whom we each are, lovingly smoothing them down and peacefully weaving them into our own inner world, the easier life flows and the clearer we become about where the voice of our True Self is calling us to go.

This book is chock-full of ideas, recommendations, skills, and strategies that can help—all of which I am constantly practicing in my own life and have witnessed having profound benefits. For the past twenty-five years, my professional work has ranged from supporting clients through the healing and dying process as an energy healer; helping writers, artists and creatives find their voice as a coach; teaching meditation and stress reduction techniques to executives and inner-city teachers; teaching classes on intuition, flow, and creative visualization; offering emotional support to clients going through transitions like midlife crises, divorce, and career changes; facilitating spiritual support and healing groups; writing and editing articles on personal growth; guiding individuals and groups through a five-step integrative coaching process I developed that helps people connect with their unique gifts and dreams called DreamCatching™; and supporting two unique and amazing children on their journeys toward adulthood, my most challenging and rewarding vocation of all.

Without question, the most important thing I've learned from all these experiences as well as my own personal growth journey is that the greatest transformation comes when we see ourselves in a new light and start applying our personal insights to our lives in our *own way*. When we meet our unique gifts, dreams, questions, imperfections, and humanity with openness and curiosity, we become able to access and implement solutions that really help our lives work.

There are several different types of prompts in this book, all of which are designed to help with this process of integration and hearing the voice of our True Selves. You can pick and choose from these prompts depending on what works best for you.

Prompt Activities

Meditation and Creative Visualization

Meditation helps us relax and more easily tap the power of our True Self, and our imagination. Creative visualization helps us tap the power of our unconscious mind to manifest change quickly, easily, and effortlessly.

Writing Exercises

Writing prompts tap both the creative and logical parts of our brain. These activities can lead us to "ah-ha" moments as well as help us figure out how to apply new insights in ways that work for us.

Art Projects

Art helps us access, explore, and experiment with the language of our intuition and True Selves, who communicate primarily through symbols and gut feelings.

Music and Movement

Music and movement are two of our most innate and ancient forms of communication. These prompts can help us tap the wealth that lies in the wisdom of our bodies.

Mindfulness Activities

Mindfulness, or being fully aware of what is happening in the present moment, provides a direct path to our peaceful, all-knowing selves, and connects us with how we are feeling right *now*.

Life Practice

Life practice prompts challenge us to apply our insights about what works best for us and see what happens.

Accelerating Change

When we first set the intention to connect with our True Selves, that decision usually happens on the mental level. We start to open to new ways of thinking about the world and our role in it, as well as new possibilities that might exist for our lives. Allowing those possibilities to manifest, however, requires more than simply intellectually accepting what our True Self has to say. When we find creative ways to engage all of who we are in the process, aligning our lives with our True Selves often happens much more easily. Throughout this book you will see that each prompt has an icon next to it. These provide an at-a-glance guide to which aspects of self each prompt is designed to engage, and a reminder that lasting transformation happens through integration and engaging all of ourselves:

☀ **Awakening Your Intuition**
One of the most powerful and least understood ways we manifest change is intuitively. Sometimes during times of transformation, it can seem as if nothing is happening from the outside, yet under the surface, we are hard at work. We may feel profound shifts as we are doing other things such as while we sleep, meditate, work, or are in a state of deep relaxation. Prompts that are designed to help us activate the power of our energy and intuition are noted with a sun icon.

♥ **Accepting Your Emotions**
When we connect with our True Selves, it is very common that we also become aware of habitual patterns, beliefs, or vulnerable emotions that might affect our ability to follow where our soft, still voice within is calling us to go. Before we take leaps, we may need to let go, heal the past, or lovingly rearrange our emotional lives to create space for what is in our highest good *now*. Prompts that can help support us in doing deep emotional healing are marked with a heart.

☑ **Aligning Your Actions**

Finally, in order to fully integrate new ideas into our lives, we need to experiment with them, and through trial and error, explore how they might work for our unique circumstances. We each need the dignity and freedom to be able to test new ideas and finetune them to see how they might best work for *us*. The more we can direct and own our own process of transformation, and the more space we can give ourselves to practice and pivot as needed, the more able we become to hear our own voice and take leaps on our own behalf. Prompts that offer opportunities for us to brainstorm practical actions, and to test these in our own lives are represented with a checkmark.

The Magic of Storytelling

Storytelling is another powerful way we integrate our own wisdom and is an important part of this book. Stories remind us how similar we all are, which can help us relax, open, and feel more connected. The state of openness we often get into when we hear or tell stories is magical. When we are in a state of feeling open and connected, we start integrating new ideas and our own wisdom in a way that can transform and change the direction of our lives. As we receive, we give; as we give, we receive. This fluidity triggers flow, a state in which new ideas and insights come, and our creativity, intuition, and compassion grow.

Quotes from Others Like *You*

This book is also filled with quotes from other intuitive creatives like *you*. These have also been included with the intention of offering encouragement, support, and inspiration, and helping to keep our energy high. No matter how much each of these creatives have achieved or how well-known they are, most likely they have experienced similar emotions and thoughts as those we are each experiencing in this very moment.

These quotes can also serve as an important reminder that we are all equal and interconnected, and that we are never alone. We can be supported and uplifted by people whom we've never met in person. You might want to imagine the authors of these quotes as members of your own personal support network —intuitive, creative friends rooting for you.

In the groups I facilitate, our motto is: *when we lift each other up, we all rise*. My hope is that by reading this book, you will feel part of a greater community and will recognize your own wisdom being echoed back to you through the words of others. My wish is that this book becomes like a beloved companion on your own journey, helping to lift you up and support you in following wherever your own soul is calling you to go.

In This Together

I am passionate about the material in this book, believe in it, and have witnessed its benefit in my own life as well as in the lives of others. I am constantly learning from everyone who comes into my life, including readers like you, and those who join me in my 28-Day Flow Challenges, groups, and workshops. I see this as a journey we are taking together—you and I as creative friends, and I am deeply grateful to have you joining me.

> "*Why should we all use our creative power? Because there is nothing that makes people so generous, joyful, lively, bold and compassionate.*"
>
> *~Barbara Ueland*

The Seven Touchstones of Creativity

When I was sixteen, I spent a summer in southern Ireland, living in an idyllic little seaside town called Greystones. The minute I arrived I felt like I was *home*. The beach was covered with small flat stones that over time had been smoothed by waves crashing against the shore. For years, I carried one of those small, flat grey stones in my pocket. This became my own personal touchstone, reminding me of what I had learned about myself and life while living in Ireland. The stone radiated an energy that felt like *me*.

As I was writing this book, I discovered that the poems that I wrote during that early 28-Day Flow Challenge fell naturally into seven categories. I call these touchstones because my hope is that the seven concepts that make up the fabric of this book will bring you the same level of comfort as the small, flat stone from Ireland did me, reminding you of who you really are and any other gifts or insights you gain on your own personal journey.

Following are the seven creative touchstones that make up the heart of this book, as well as some tips to help you deepen your journey through the pages ahead.

#1: Inspiration

Your joy connects you with your True Self

I believe life is filled with invitations to experience joy and goodness, regardless of outer events that might feel like they are happening *to* us. Sometimes connecting with our joy is more challenging than others. It might feel like a huge departure from how we have lived our lives in the past, or what we think we *should* be doing. Other times, prioritizing our joy comes more easily. Either way, joy can be a powerful touchstone, leading us to a sense of peace, purpose, strength, and comfort.

Tip: Celebrate what brings YOU joy

As you find your way through this book, you might want to think about how to integrate a simple joyful activity into your daily routine, ideally, something you don't already do. Your daily activity doesn't have to be creative or related to your favorite hobby. For example, if you consider yourself to be a poet or want to be, you don't have to choose writing poetry as your daily practice. The key is, does it bring you joy? Does it boost your confidence? Does it help you stay inspired? Does it help you connect with that part of you that is always peaceful and filled with wonder and possibilities? It is in joyful moments that we most easily connect with our inner guidance about what is best for us and our lives.

#2: Process

You have a unique process for getting life to flow

We are all creative, and we each have our own best way of reaching our goals, experiencing love, joy, and creative flow. We often receive the message that something is wrong with us if a system developed for someone else doesn't work for *us*. Life becomes a lot more interesting when we start to experiment, uncover, and honor the unique creative processes that *do* work for us. The question isn't whether we are creative, it's how we can tap the genius that is inherent within each of us, each in our own unique way.

Tip: Honor what works for YOU

Each time I facilitate a group, there are some who are more apt to get personal insights or into a state of creative flow in the middle of the night; others say their inner voice seems to speak most loudly first thing in the morning; many thrive on repetition and regular schedules; still others find their lives work best when they build in lots of flexibility, giving themselves lots of space and freedom so they can follow their intuition and go with life's flow.

The key to getting life to flow and finding your own personal way of traveling through the pages of this book is honoring *your* natural creative rhythm. Trust how you learn and work best, and your own unique formula for connecting with your inner voice and following where it leads.

#3: Blocks

Everything that happens offers gifts

Life can be messy and unpredictable. We have all, at one time or another, been negatively impacted in some way by those things we can't control—like hurtful words or actions of others, death or illness, unexpected change, or not being fully supported in a way that works best for *us*. Because blocks and pain are part of the human story, they are also part of our power. As we practice accepting the positive and challenging aspects of ourselves and our lives, we start realizing that we can use everything that happens to us to create something new and beautiful. Learning to work with rather than against our emotional blocks can help our creativity, intuition, and our hearts to expand.

Tip: Respect your blocks

We all have things that trigger us or that make our lives particularly challenging. Finding out what our unique triggers and challenges are, and how to keep our creative flow going when we feel blocked can be deeply personal. We may think something is wrong with us, or that we need to get rid of whatever is making us feel blocked with willpower, muscle, or sheer brute strength. The truth is that feeling blocked is as much a natural part of life as is creating.

Creating is very much like the birthing process. Whenever we are making a change, changing a habit, or birthing something new in our lives, we will have times of great openings, and other times where we feel a sense of restriction, or our flow being blocked. The more we understand how normal blocks can be, the less panicked we become when they happen to us, and the more able we become to work with our blocks rather than against them.

Sometimes feeling blocked is simply a sign that we need to wait and let the natural course of events to unfold. Other times, blocks might be a sign that we need to make minor adjustments to our creative processes or rhythms—*how* we do our work, our mindset, or our attitude toward how we believe we should be living our lives. Other times blocks may be emotional in nature and linked to our beliefs about ourselves and our abilities, forgotten emotional pain, our unique DNA, or trauma - whether our own, or traumas experienced within our family lineage that continue to have an impact on how we experience the world.

Creative flow doesn't happen through avoiding our imperfections or what makes us uncomfortable. Rather, the key to flow is gathering all of that to us like a mother would her young, unruly children, knowing that our True Self is powerful enough to welcome and love it all.

It's so important to respect our emotional blocks. Our deepest wounds are often invisible. Sometimes we are not even aware they exist until they get unexpectedly retriggered by outer events. If you feel like you are at an impasse in your life, or are feeling stuck or a particularly big reaction or emotion, it can be very important to reach out for support. Emotional blocks and insecure feelings are completely natural, part of the human experience. At some point, we have all had to get help in figuring out what is getting in the way of us taking our next best step forward.

Examples of professionals who may help us move through blocks include therapists, life coaches, creativity coaches, energy healers, mental health experts, medical professionals, sports coaches trained in the mind-body connection, body workers, acupuncturists, cranial sacral therapists, spiritual teachers, or other professionals well-versed in the relationship between trauma, creativity, stress, anxiety, and our mental, emotional, and physical well-being, or trustworthy family members or friends. The most important thing in seeking help is to make sure you feel safe enough with whomever you have chosen to support you to be honest and authentic about how you are feeling and what you are experiencing.

Vulnerability is paramount when it comes to emotional healing, and therapists, physicians, ministers, and spiritual professionals are all human too. If you feel judged or as if you can't fully be yourself with someone, most likely they are not the ideal person with whom to process your blocks at this time. Our needs are constantly changing and evolving. Finding someone whose vantage point and energy resonate with yours at this current time in your life is important. Just because someone has professional credentials or has helped us in the past doesn't automatically qualify them to work with us and our unique set of challenges in the present. Sometimes, healers have a preconceived notion of what healing looks like, who we are, or who they are supposed to be that can get in the way of our healing, no matter how well-intentioned they may be.

Rarely can one person meet all our needs in any area of our lives, and that includes emotional and creative support. Most of us benefit from relying on a team of close friends, teachers, family members, and professionals. There is a huge number of people in the world sharing diverse gifts and offering support, through a wide variety of means including podcasts, books, online classes, groups, and private therapeutic sessions. It's also important to remember that there is no such thing as a perfect anything, and that includes therapists, teachers, and mentors. Mental health and creativity professionals have their own blocks, distraction, prejudices, and cultural upbringing, all of which color the work that they do, no matter how well-trained or how much work they have done on themselves. A relationship with a therapist, physician, teacher, healer, or coach doesn't have to be perfect for us to still experience benefits. Our well-being should come before our desire to find the perfect person to help us achieve it.

Personally, I think the most gifted healers are those who are continually and actively doing their own inner work behind the scenes. The more comfortable they are with their own dark places, the easier it is for them to hold space for others to do the same in a safe and supportive way. A safe person from whom to seek support is open, genuinely wants the very best for you, and shows great respect and confidence in *you, your* intuition, wisdom, and ability to heal, create, and share valuable gifts with the world.

#4: Life

Your life is filled with miracles

Sometimes, we are so focused on what is next, or on what we want to create, experience, or become that we forget how much power there is in the present moment. We are constantly creating and evolving. We are not the same people we were one minute ago, let alone one year ago. The key to unlocking our unique creative energy is realizing and fully participating in the magic of creation happening within and all around us. In other words, there is nothing we need to do to receive life's creative magic. It already belongs to us, no matter who we are.

Tip: Share who you really are

If we really want to find and follow our creative voice, it often works best when we bring the rest of our lives along with us. A common belief is that we need to keep the many different areas of our work and personal lives, such as family, marriage, fitness, career, friendships, travel, etc., in separate balanced categories. The thinking is that when one area of overflows, it squashes others.

When we integrate who we really are in all areas of our lives with a sense of self-acceptance, peace, sharing, and receiving, rather than feeling an inner sense of war or conflict, things really start to move forward in a positive way. Leaping is about aligning what we do with who we are and where our inner voice is guiding us to go. It's also about making peace with the areas of our lives where this is more difficult or not yet possible.

#5: Circles

You have infinite support

Most of us spend a lot of our time with the same people and doing the same things we've always done. We can forget how expansive the world is, and how many different possibilities exist for our lives. Most people in the world are genuinely good and want the same things we want—to be loved, appreciated, seen, accepted, and to share and receive life's gifts. Whenever we least expect it, loving support appears, often in a form we could never have anticipated. The question isn't whether support exists, it's how we can keep our energy bright so that we recognize and find that support and see our way forward on the paths that are right for each of us.

Tip: Stay open

On any significant journey, it helps when we have fellow travelers to keep us company. The key here is with whom do you resonate? What energy makes you feel safe? What kind of gifts do you admire in others? What inspires you? Your circle might be made up of real people—friends, loved ones, family members, or creative peers, or even past teachers, mentors, or cheerleaders - the memory of whom keeps you going on the path that is right for *you*. Building a circle is about finding people who inspire you, who bring out the best in you, with whom you can really be yourself. It can also be made up of people you don't even know or never will in person—famous artists or painters whose work you follow, learn about, and keep alive in your daily life in some way.

Relationships are how we practice important skills like acceptance, openness, giving and receiving, creation, and love. They are also how we see more clearly where we are blocked and where we are ready to grow. The key is keeping our relationships with those who uplift us active and a priority. Healthy relationships where there is enough space for both parties to shine offer a pathway by which we can strengthen our relationships with ourselves. Nurturing our intuition and creativity means asking for support when we need it while also trusting our own inner wisdom. The more we do this, the more likely we are to meet and connect with others who have similar desires, needs, gifts and perspectives, and who can support us on a higher path. It's equally important to share our gifts as it is to be open to others' gifts, and to accept inspiration and support from many different sources. This can mean connecting in person, or rereading, revisiting, and remembering all those whose teachings and works resonate and uniquely inspire us. In the absence of real people, teachers from afar can also help to serve the need we all have for connection and support.

I have also noticed that the more we show up when people in our circles take intuitive and creative risks, the more our own intuition and creativity seem to expand. Cheer on your friends. Find other creative, intuitive, and inspiring souls who are generous, confident, and truly want the very best for you without seeing it as jeopardizing their own progress or path. You can tell whether this is true by how you feel.

The key is allowing our circles to be fluid and inclusive with a true spirit of give and take. If we feel like we are taking more than we are giving, or like someone else is pulling our energy down instead of lifting us up, this usually means we need to allow more space—space in which that new just-right friend will soon appear, or that will allow for clearer seeing. Sometimes our existing relationships need more space so that both parties can grow, expand, and evolve. Ultimately, the most important thing when it comes to circles is remembering that we are the only person responsible for our own well-being. Honoring our own truth and taking loving care of ourselves is good for us all.

Our circles can be wide and we can travel in many different circles. We can find supportive, caring, intuitive, creative friends on social media, or the Internet, by joining creative or spiritual groups or classes, by seeking others on similar journeys or those with a similar perspective or vibe as our own. You might also think of me, other readers of this book, and the creatives who are quoted throughout its pages as members of your tribe, voices from a larger, loving web that is energetically and invisibly supporting you on your own unique journey.

#6: Callings

You have unique gifts to offer the world

Life is filled with endless opportunities to experience miracles and to create new things. Whenever we feel overwhelmed with trying to figure out where to put our energy, it can help to reconnect with that soft, still voice, guiding us in even the most mundane and minor decisions. The more comfortable we become with our own experience of answers not being readily apparent *out there*, the more receptive we become to hearing our own whispers within.

Tip: Listen for your truth

We rarely know the full impact of our journey on earth. We may think we are giving people one gift, and we are leaving them with something else entirely. We inspire others through our actions or, as Maya Angelou said so beautifully, "how you made them feel."

Our own personal life journeys are creative entities unto themselves; the ways in which we honor our own creative voice, stand in our truth, and put ourselves out into the world often have a reach far beyond what we could ever fathom. Hearing our intuitive callings is as much about having the wisdom, space, confidence, and fortitude to support and cheer on others on their journeys as it is about tuning into and trusting the voice of our True Selves.

#7: Your Next Leap

You will be ready when it's time

The purpose of our lives is not just about the big leaps we take, it's also about the small leaps that no one else will ever know about. No matter what is happening in the outer world, nothing can ever change the power of your inner light. By staying with the power of our own inner voice, we each will discover that we have everything we need to get our lives flowing in exciting new directions. If you are feeling called to create something new or make a change, you already have what you need and will know when it's time.

Tip: Trust your creative voice

This book is not just about finding time and space in which to create and nurture our relationships with our inner voices, it is also about knowing when it's time to leap in a new direction. Sometimes when to the outward world, it might look as if we are stuck or not fully sharing our gifts, we may be in the process of coming up with something new, allowing an unconscious idea to marinate and incubate until it's ready to take hold. Beneath the surface, we are forming a strong foundation against which to push off when it's time to leap.

As you read this book and live your life, trust your own process and ideas. You might want to jot down seemingly-random thoughts or insights that come to you. You also might highlight or circle words or phrases in this book that seem to jump off the page. These could be signs as to where your True Self is calling you next. The more we recognize and honor our own creative voice and intuitive leadings, the more quickly life starts to change, often in miraculous ways. My hope is that as you follow where your own true voice is calling you, you'll feel like you are being supported by a greater creative community, cheering you on every step of the way.

"Trust that when you're ready to let go, your wings will discover themselves."

~ Emily Ruth Hazel

When we lift each other up,
we all rise.

The Seven Touchstones of Creativity

Inspiration

What inspires you?

When I was young, I spent most of my summers walking around barefoot. I also got lots of bee stings, poor honeybees engorging themselves on clover flowers who weren't expecting to die so young between the dirty toes of a small inquisitive girl.

One hot summer night, I was on my typical warpath, walking in my favorite denim shorts and t-shirt through the long, green grass of our yard when I experienced something I had never before.

I was standing on tiptoe, teetering at the edge of my mother's iris garden, a cacophony of beautiful blooms in a smattering of colors and with names equally as beautiful.

My mother's gardens were like so much of what she created—antique blue vases lined up on windowsills; hand-sewn, ruffly throw pillows; fresh-baked blueberry muffins in baskets with blue calico napkins—a backdrop to our young lives, silently grounding us like a canvas does paints.

On that hot summer night, I leaned in to smell a yellow blossom. I just wanted a whiff of its sweet scent and to see if I could spot the intricate black design in the center, tucked between the curling petals.

That's when I saw it, out of the corner of my eye. It was iridescent green with wings that went so fast, I was sure it was some sort of alien bee. As soon as I looked up, it was gone.

I wanted to tell someone, to find out if anyone else had seen it or if there was anyone who could confirm that I had, indeed, just witnessed a miracle. But there was no one else around.

Looking back, I now realize I must have seen a hummingbird for the very first time. While it wasn't an alien bee, and there were lots more hummingbirds in the world, my younger self was right about one thing. I had seen something that no one in the entire world ever had or would again. No one else would ever see that hummingbird in that exact way or know what it felt like to be me at that particular moment in time.

This is the reality of what it means to be creative—we are constantly being offered gifts and having insights that are different than what anyone else is experiencing. We each have our own unique filters through which we come to know and share the beauty and challenges that collectively we call life. The job of sharing our own unique perspective and version of this collective story belongs to us and us alone.

The key to finding our unique message, our unique gifts, I believe, begins with restoring our sense of wonder and inspiration. Wonder and inspiration occur when the conditions are just right. We are in the right place in the right time. We have the open eyes, hearts, and minds of small children. We let ourselves be taken in, then taken for a ride. We allow ourselves to be toppled off balance, caught off-guard, and surprised. We realize, in that moment, that what we have witnessed is a gift for us and us alone to share with the world in our own time, in our own unique way.

Whatever passes our path is ours to use, to fold into a story decades later, to mull over and find some wisdom that surpasses time. Whether we are artists, writers, poets, photographers, dreamers, bakers and iris planters like my mother, or simply curious wanderers like my child self, the world is our canvas, our palette of paints, our own personal pot of poetic prompts, free for the taking.

And take it we do. We take it all in, work with it in the way only we can, then share it with those who were busy with other things at the time, doing our best to describe what just happened and how we've been changed.

No matter what our unique path is, one thing is sure. The things we don't yet know are as important as those we do. Ignorance and curiosity impact our way of seeing far more than all those things we know for sure.

When we find the courage to look beyond our assumptions about ourselves, others and the world, and share what we've discovered in a state of curiosity and inspiration, we merge with all the other mysteries in the universe, becoming active players in their unfolding.

> *"I believe we are all capable at times of brushing up against a sense of mystery and inspiration in our lives."*
>
> *~Elizabeth Gilbert*

Leap with Me

Breathe with me now,
says the Darkness
in her most hushed voice.
I look to see
to whom she is speaking,
but see no one else
but me.

Fly with me now,
calls the Moonlight.
Soar with me to
far-off lands
Let your Lightness
carry you to the sea.

Trust me now,
screeches the Owl,
crying through the night.
As you hear me,
I see you.

Unwrap me now,
pleads Wisdom,
those quiet words
landing upon
my mind,
a last offering of
the day's gifts.

Leap with me now,
invites my Heart
as she yearns
to stretch farther,
to travel
far away from me
to her other Self, out there.

You have become
more alive
Today
than you ever were,
I hear,
as I call back
to the whispers
with a hushed:
"I hear you."

With those three little words,
a cacophony of sparks,
an explosion of happiness
for this –
the awakening
of all that we are,
you and I –
connecting
just for an instant
with all that is.

Prompt ~ Unwrap Your Gift ☀

Meditation + Writing Activity
Tools: A quiet, private place, your *Leap Journal*, and a pen
Time: Approximately 10 minutes

Before we begin any journey, it can be helpful to set an intention as to where we want to go, and what we want to experience along the way. As we begin this adventure together, find a comfortable place to take a few minutes just for you. Ask yourself:

What do I most need and want right now?

- Take a nice deep breath.

- Close your eyes and imagine being in a safe place. This might be in nature, or a special room or shelter created just for you.

- Now imagine a close friend, imaginary friend, or someone who knows you well arrives there holding a gift, decorated in a way that makes it clear this gift is for *you*.

- Your friend tells you this gift is something that can help you more easily achieve what you really need and want at this point in your life.

- It includes a card that says: *Unwrap Me Now*. What's inside?

Our intuition communicates in the form of symbols, simple sentences, colors, and feelings. Trust what comes to you, knowing it doesn't have to make sense. If nothing comes, that's okay—make something up! This gift can be your own personal touchstone, like that small stone from Ireland I used to keep in my pocket, reminding you what you most want to create as you navigate the pages of this book.

Prompt ~ Receive Your Gift ☀

Art Project
Tools: Your *Leap Journal*, colored pencils, or crayons
Time: Approximately 10 minutes

For this prompt, choose the gift you received in the previous visualization, or choose a new one by asking yourself:

> *What gift, symbol, or word represents what I want*
> *my relationship with my true inner voice to be like?*

- Sketch your gift, focusing on how you feel as you are creating.
- Post your sketch somewhere you spend time regularly, like your sink or mirror, in your wallet, on your bedside table, desk, or car dashboard. You could also take a digital photo of your sketch and make it your computer screensaver or background on your phone.
- Another way to do this prompt is to find an actual item, like a shell, rock, or treasure from nature, or buy yourself a gift that reflects the energy of what you want your relationship with your True Self to be like, and what you want to experience on this creative journey.

Prompt ~ Becoming More Alive ☀

Writing Exercise
Tools: A private place, your *Leap Journal*, and a pen
Time: Approximately 15 minutes

Those moments when we feel really *alive* can be a message from our True Selves, guiding us to choose activities and experiences that are aligned with who we really are.

In your *Leap Journal*, jot down words or phrases that answer the following questions:

- What are some moments when you have felt really *alive*?
- What is something you could do right now that might help you to feel *more alive*?

To take this prompt deeper, complete the following sentences. Keep your pen moving, writing whatever comes to you.

- I feel joy when I …
- This really fills me with passion…
- I feel inspired when…
- To me, feeling really *alive* means...

Write Your Own Poem

Want to take this prompt deeper? Rearrange the phrases from your answers and string them together in a poem about becoming *more alive*.

> *"Don't worry about what the world needs. Ask what makes you come alive and do that, because what the world needs is people who have come alive."*
>
> *~Howard Thurman*

What Moves You?

I ask you,
just this once –
what moves you?

What takes your heart
and shakes it up,
shattering around
all the pieces
so the unwanted ones
fall to the ground
like rubble
and dust
never to be repeated
or welcomed back?

What does that –
that great clearing
that wakes you up
and makes space
for Lightness,
emerging New Life
like butterflies
circling out of crusty chrysalises
ready for new flight?

What makes you feel like that?
I ask,
feeling rather proud of myself
like a three-year old who is so
full of her own Selfness
that she stands up tall
and struts with a posture
that cannot be taught
and comes from the inside
as she at first grasps
that she is owned
only by herself.

Because you see,
I know things move us
like that
because I was so moved
once
or twice.

Granted, it happened
in the middle of the night
when I cried and cried myself to sleep,
feeling as if I was missing out,
as if life was passing me by,
as if I had achieved some great error
that could not be erased
until I was.

But, you see, I was not writing then.

Now what moves me
are words,
ever so quiet,
words.

I am settling in.

I don't know how or why it happened,
but something went off inside me.

I realized then,
there doesn't have to be
so much
fanfare
around a miracle.

Prompt ~ What Moves You? ☀

Movement Exercise
Tools: A quiet, private place, music, your *Leap Journal,* and a pen
Time: Approximately three minutes

Movement can be a very powerful tool in learning to create our own mini mood-turnarounds throughout the day. In this exercise, you will need a private space and some uplifting music.

- Take a nice deep breath.
- As you listen to the music, let your body move however you feel led.
- If at any point you feel stuck, ask yourself: *What takes your heart and shakes it up?*
- Invite your body to tell its own personal *shake it up* story.
- With each movement, imagine you are letting go of any energy that no longer reflects who you are.
- Move in whatever way best allows your True Self to emerge.
- Trust your intuition to lead you.

After completing this prompt, notice if you experience any changes in how you feel. Record any "ah-has" in your *Leap Journal.*

Prompt ~ Miracle Mandala ☀

Art Project
Tools: *Leap Journal*, colored magic markers, glue sticks, and scissors
Time: Approximately 45 minutes

Have you ever experienced something that helped you feel *full of your own Selfness,* sacredness, or divinity? For this prompt, we are going to combine a Mind Map, a common brainstorming technique, with collaging to create our own personal Miracle Mandalas.

If you've never created a Mind Map before, here's the basic idea.

- Write the word *Miracle* in the center of a page from your *Leap Journal*. Draw a circle around it, as if it is a sun.

- Set a timer for three minutes.

- Try to think of as many words or simple phrases that to you represent what a Miracle means. Each time you think of a new word, draw a line coming from the word Miracle, and then write the new word at the end of it, as if each new word is a ray of light shining out from the center of the sun. You might choose to circle these new words too.

- If you think of a word related to the last one you wrote, keep extending the line further and further, adding new related words as you go. When you think of a word that takes you on a new tangent, begin at the center again. Don't overthink this, it's simply a brainstorming technique. There is no right or wrong way to do this.

- After your three minutes are up, look at what you've written. Do any of your new words jump out at you? Circle them with a magic marker in your favorite color.

Option ~ One Step Further

- Now find some old magazines.
- Set a timer for seven minutes.
- Go through the magazines and tear out random images and words that to you represent the energy of a Miracle or any of the other words that appeared on your Mind Map.
- When you are done, get a new, blank piece of paper, either from your *Leap Journal*, or perhaps a larger piece of poster board, construction paper, or plain white printer paper, and cut out and arrange your words and images in a circular pattern, creating your very own Miracle Mandala.
- Your mandala can reveal the unique gifts and miraculous healing essence you have to offer the world.
- You might put this mandala somewhere you see often, or even use it as a focal point for your very own *Miracle Meditation.*
- This meditation can be as simple as focusing on your Miracle Mandala while imagining all the miracles you have already received in your life and saying prayer of thanks. You could also request or set an intention for your own personal transformation, turn-around, or miraculous shift in perspective.

Prompt ~ Advice from a Miraculous Friend ☑

Meditation and Writing Exercise
Tools: A quiet, private place, your *Leap Journal*, and a pen
Time: Approximately 10 minutes + one week

When people have profound, life-changing experiences, the positive energy they experience as a result often filters out to benefit others as well. We can invite change in our lives by learning from others who know firsthand what a miracle feels like through the power of our imagination.

- Close your eyes and pretend you are watching a movie on a screen.

- Imagine a fictitious character experiencing a miraculous event, personal transformation, or shift in consciousness.

- Imagine that the movie pauses at a key moment, and you get to have a conversation with the lead character.

- What guidance might this character have for you and your life? Let the conversation unfold spontaneously, as if you are playing make-believe. It's okay to make this up as you go along. If you find creative visualization challenging, you could write this as a fictional story in your *Leap Journal* instead.

- After you feel complete, slowly open your eyes, and write the advice this fictitious character offered you in your *Leap Journal*.

- Try out the advice you received for one week and see what happens.

> *"We forget that the inner value – the rapture that is associated with being alive, is what it's all about."*
>
> ~*Joseph Campbell*

Joy Bank

They think I've lost
my sense of adventure
as I shy away from ice cold plunges,
one toe touching the lapping waves

Tentatively.

They pity me as I say,
"Go on without me"
as they venture on high seas and
tall peaks.

They wonder,
"Was she ever fun?"

And I smile gently,
remembering
my own daring adventures,
bottled up in my heart,
feeding me even now.

I can't tell them
as they look,
seeing my youth fading,
about how grateful I am
that they are taking risks
and living
and soaking up
all life has to offer.

I can't tell them, yet,
how memories,
locked within my heart,
are a Joy Bank

from which I reap dividends
as I do exactly what it is
I most want to do
Now
(and exactly, as it turns out,
what those dividends are really for)
and write,
write and
write.

They can't understand yet,
that this,
my new
Solo Mission,
the act of
unveiling and creating,
dipping my pen into
Past Plunges
is by far
the most
Daring Adventure
of
them
all.

Prompt ~ What's in Your Joy Bank? 

Writing Exercise
Tools: Your *Leap Journal*, a pen, and a friend
Time: Approximately 20 minutes (and ongoing)

I believe we each have an inner *Joy Bank* filled with happy memories that remind us who we really are. When we focus on what we love and what brings us joy, we activate a positive energy that can uplift and support us through tough times, as well as that can flow out and positively affect others as well. This prompt is about brainstorming the contents of your own personal Joy Bank. (This exercise can be a great conversation starter. You might want to share what's in your Joy Bank with a friend.)

Sometimes when we have difficult experiences, we can get stuck in seeing things from a negative perspective. This prompt can help us remember good times and provide a path for keeping these as our focus as we move forward in creating new ones. How we remember the past and what we choose to focus on can affect our future choices, and even our identity and how we view ourselves.

Option 1 ~ Happy Memories

- What are those happiest memories or experiences that are still giving you positive energy, just waiting to be tapped again? Make a list. Your Joy Bank might include major milestones like a favorite trip, your wedding day, or special celebration. It could also include memories of tasting a favorite meal, watching a sunset, going for a swim, feeling the warmth of sunlight. Look through your list as if you are a detective, looking for themes or a specific formula regarding what brings you joy.

Ask yourself the five W questions—who, what, where, why, and when.

- **Who** were you with in your happiest memories?
- **What** were you doing?
- **Where** did your joyful memories happen?
- **Why** were you doing these things?
- **When** did your memories happen? (What time of day, season, etc.)

Option 2 ~ Things That Make You Smile

If you're having trouble accessing happy memories, no worries. Our Joy Banks can also include any items that bring us joy like a favorite color, a song, book, hobby, food, loved ones, or dreams for the future.

- Make a list of everything that brings you joy. For extra inspiration, leaf through magazines, social media, or online images. Whenever you see something that makes you smile, add it to your Joy Bank list.

Option 3 ~ Making Joy Deposits

Every time we experience joy, it's as if we make a deposit we can draw on in the future.

- Start tracking your joyful experiences.
- Bookmark this page of your *Leap Journal*.
- Keep updating and expanding your list.

Going Deeper

Did you gain any new "ah-has" about what brings you joy, or how you *do* joy that can apply to your current life? What do the items or memories in your Joy Bank have in common? Circle themes. Write down your insights.

Prompt ~ Joy Bank Collage ☀

Art Project
Tools: Blank paper, photos, old magazines scissors, glue sticks, or tape
Time: Approximately 20 minutes

This prompt takes this idea of each of us having our own personal *Joy Bank* one step further. The underlying idea is that when we think about things that bring us joy, we often start radiating positive energy that can attract similar positive joyful experiences and opportunities to us.

I believe what brings us joy is a clue, leading us to the unique gifts and energy we have to offer the world.

Create a collage filled with images that bring you joy and make you smile. See how you feel as you do this prompt, and how looking at what you create makes you feel afterwards.

- Find photos that represent some of your happiest moments.
- Leaf through old magazines and find images that bring you joy.
- Arrange these images on a piece of paper in a way that pleases you.
- Attach them with glue or tape.

Post what you create in a place where you will see it often, like your refrigerator door, bathroom mirror, bedroom, or office.

Prompt ~ Take a Daring Adventure ☑

Writing Exercise
Tools: Your *Leap Journal*, and a pen
Time: Approximately 10 minutes + one week

What's a leap, *Daring Adventure,* or *Solo Mission* you'd like to take in your life? Examples might be a creative venture you've been dreaming about, new hobby you'd like to try, friendship you'd like to create, or relationship you'd like to take to the next level. Your *Daring Adventure* could also be a vacation you want to take, or even something more subtle like a small step in your own healing or transformation.

- In your *Leap Journal,* make a list of possible *Daring Adventures.*

- Choose your favorite one and write a poem or story about how you will feel when you are on that adventure.

- What is one realistic small step you can take today to begin your next *Daring Adventure*? Write it down in your calendar.

- After you've taken the first step, describe how you feel in your *Leap Journal*. Choose your next step and write that in your calendar. Keep leaping!

> "*Life is either a daring adventure, or nothing.*"
>
> *~Hellen Keller*

Overflowing

I am hopeless
some days
at getting anything done.

It's flowing out of me,
these words.

Like a bathtub overflowing,
all I can do
is stand there
flabbergasted
by the show,
not knowing what to do.

So I put a pot out
to catch the drips

Because I really
don't want to
turn off the faucet.

Prompt ~ Your Inner Rhythm☀

Mindfulness Activity
Tools: You!
Time: One minute (or longer)

There is often a creative rhythm or voice humming along beneath the surface of our lives. However, we may not be aware of it unless we take the time to listen.

- Take a deep breath and sit quietly for a moment.
- Notice how you are feeling.
- Pay attention to your body.
- Keep breathing and do whatever you can to deeply relax.
- See if there, underneath the surface of what you usually pay attention to, is something else. It might feel like an energy moving, a quiet awareness, or even a loving voice.
- Just pay attention, without trying to make it into anything.
- Just notice.

The more we tune in, the more we become aware of this energy, almost as if it is beckoning to us to pay attention.

Prompt ~ Behind the Scenes ♥

Art Project
Tools: Crayons, two blank pieces of paper, and a timer
Time: Approximately 10 minutes

Research by Lucia Capacchione, author of *The Power of Your Other Hand,* suggests that writing with our non-dominant hand can help us unlock the intuitive wisdom of our Truest Selves.

For this prompt, we are going to use our non-dominant hand. (For example, if you are right-handed, use your left hand, or if you are left-handed, use your right hand.)

- Think of a time when you were hopeless at getting anything done or felt stuck in your life.

- Set a timer for ten minutes.

- *Ask yourself:* What inner work might you have been doing behind the scenes?

- With your non-dominant hand, draw a picture of what might have been happening under the surface that you may not have realized at the time. Let your inner self choose the colors and draw the picture, as if it is a young child.

The goal is to get out of the way and let this inner child create. This exercise is not about making fine art, it's about tapping that intuitive part of you that is always working for your highest good and trying to communicate with you. As with all prompts in this book, the quality of what you create is not important, instead what matters is how you *feel* as you do this exercise.

Prompt ~ Drawing Now ☀

Art Project + Mindfulness Activity
Tools: Crayons, two blank pieces of paper, and a timer
Time: Approximately 10 minutes

This prompt is like the previous one except instead of focusing on a time in the past, we are going to use the power of our non-dominant hands to help us become more intuitively aware of what's happening in the present moment.

- Set a timer for 10 minutes.

- Take a few nice deep breaths.

- Notice how you feel.

- Using your non-dominant hand, draw a picture that depicts what is going on with you in this moment. Where is your energy blocked? Where and how are you letting the energy of your True Self flow?

- Ask your inner child artist:

What's really going on?

What might help?

- Let your inner child show you what they want you to know.

When you are complete, look at your art and see if you have any new insights. Write them down in your *Leap Journal.*

Prompt ~ Catching Drips ☑

Writing Exercise
Tools: Your *Leap Journal* and a pen
Time: Approximately 10 minutes + one week

Intuitive information is always available to us. We might think of this like the mist of fog, it's all around us. We might be so used to this intuitive mist that we take it for granted, or not even realize it's there. Change happens, often very quickly, when we realize that we can capture drops from this intuitive, creative mist at any time to make our lives better.

- Set your timer for 10 minutes.
- Take a deep breath and tune into the energy around you.
- *Ask yourself:* What is true in this moment? Make a list of everything that comes to mind even if it seems to have nothing to do with you.
- *Next, ask:* What, in this moment, is calling me? What is boosting my energy? Write it all down.
- When the timer goes off, look over your lists. What are some simple action steps you could take this week to stay connected to the positive energy you felt during this exercise? Write down your ideas. Try one out this week.

> *"The painting has a life of its own. I try to let it come through."*
>
> *~Jackson Pollock*

May I, Please?

May I, please, have a moment?
Just a second,
before you interrupt?

To capture this fragment
a wisp
flitting away
in my psyche

Just there,
past my thoughts
about how to walk forward
and what's on my to-do list

May I please, just?
I gasp as words from their lips start,
crowding the words
in my mind.

Just,
if you don't mind,
I stutter,
hand out
palm flat outward,
stopping signal
that motion,
the one we all know in any language.

Go no further.
Stop where you are.
No trespassing past here.

So rude, they think
and I do too.

Too harsh.
So hard.
If only!

They so want to
tell me that more important thing

And I stand,
dejected as they do,
and the words
offered up
in my mind
disappear

Like a magical visitor,
an elf or fairy,
darting across
the street or train tracks
as a powerful locomotive
powers through.

I can't reach you
Where did you go?
I whisper, while listening
to my real-world friend
or neighbor
or loved one,
trying to be polite.

Yet inwardly,
I feel such
great loss
for yet another fragment,
yet another word
gone missing,
never to return.

She might come back, of course.

But next time,
instead of her pink flowing fairy dress,
she might be wearing blue

And as she twirls in the moonlight
she will look
just a tad different
than she would have
if I had captured her
when she was going
by another name.

Prompt ~ Boundary Brainstorm ☑

Writing Exercise
Tools: Your *Leap Journal*, a pen, and a friend
Time: Approximately 20 minutes + one week

The more attuned we become to our intuitive and creative inner voice, the more frustrated we may become by outer distractions.

Answer the following questions in your *Leap Journal*. Make a list, brainstorming your options.

- What frequently distracts you from doing things that inspire you?

- What's a compassionate request you could make or way you could create a firm boundary against these distractions, that wouldn't disrupt your life too much?

Choose one idea that appeals to you the most. This week, experiment with implementing your idea and see what happens. Take notes about what happens and how you feel in your *Leap Journal*. Share your insights with a friend.

Prompt ~ Magical Visitors ☀

Meditation
Tools: Your *Leap Journal* and a pen
Time: Approximately 20 minutes

We often know far more than we realize about the creative callings and insights tugging at our hearts.

Close your eyes for a few minutes.

- If you were being visited by *magical visitors of inspiration* right now or in your dreams, what forms might these be taking?
- Invite a few of these magical visitors to meet with you in your imagination. It helps to get in a deeply relaxed state before doing this exercise. (If you find this challenging, make something up!)
- What might these magical visitors want you to know?
- What are they asking of you?
- What wisdom or gifts have they come to offer you?

Write down whatever information comes to you in this meditation in your *Leap Journal*.

Prompt ~ Too Harsh ♥

Writing Exercise
Tools: Your *Leap Journal*, pen, and timer
Time: Approximately 20 minutes

Staying inspired can require protecting ourselves from those things that get in the way. Setting boundaries is a skill like any other. We learn by being willing to be beginners, make mistakes, and do it imperfectly.

For this prompt, write a story about a time when you or someone else set a boundary and it didn't go well.

The important thing for this prompt is to keep your pen moving. Just get all your ideas down on paper. Don't worry about whether your story is well-written or even true. We are simply going to explore our feelings and what we have come to believe about boundaries.

Often issues related to boundaries can trigger challenging emotions like shame, anger, vulnerability, or fear. This prompt is about softening all of that and simply exploring the idea of setting boundaries by engaging the joyful power of our imagination. Once we let go and start to play with creativity, setting boundaries can seem a lot less serious and can actually be fun!

- Set a timer for 20 minutes.

- Write your "boundary setting event" on the top of the page. If this were a fictional story, what might a good title for it be?

- You can write your story in first person (I…) or third person (She/he/they…). You can also use this prompt to tell another person's boundary story.

- Why did you/they need to set a boundary?
- How did you/they try to do this?
- How did each character in the story respond to the boundaries that were or weren't set?
- What went well?
- What didn't?
- What were the short-term and long-term consequences of the choices made?
- What is another way this story could have gone? Write an alternate happy ending. Have fun imagining what could have gone differently, or how you would have liked the story to go.
- Another option for this prompt is to write a humorous *bad* ending. How could this boundary setting story have gone even worse than what happened in real life? Enjoy!

> "*Compassionate people have boundaries. Boundaries are a way to support your life.*"
>
> ~*Koren Motekaitis*

Beautiful Distractions

I don't care about my writing
being good
or grammatically correct,
or when to dot the i
or use a semicolon.

All I care about is how to get these thoughts
cluttering my mind
blocking my view
filling my every thought,
out of my way
so that I can see clearly
and focus
on the moment.

They collide like ping pong balls
or too many pinballs
ricocheting
against each other
like drunken lost souls.

Creative sparks,
they just want to be captured

Tantalizingly teasing
and tempting me

Threatening to combust into dust and disappear
if I don't give them attention.

Unruly beautiful children
not yet birthed,
ideas that just want to find their way to the page
before they disappear forever.

I see them, hear them laughing,
beckoning me,
filling my everywhere

Doing everything in their power
to get me to come and play

As I stand before the
open refrigerator
trying to decide
what to make for dinner.

Prompt ~ Drunken Lost Souls ☀

Mindfulness Activity
Tools: A private space, a timer, your *Leap Journal,* and a pen
Time: Five minutes

For this prompt, we are going to explore the messages, themes, symbols, colors, characters, or ideas that keep popping up again and again in our lives or creative work, almost like unruly children begging for our attention.

- Set your timer for five minutes.
- Close your eyes.
- Take a few nice deep breaths.
- See if you can capture the thoughts and sparks of inspiration flitting about in your imagination, as if simply witnessing them is the ultimate achievement, rather than making sense out of what you notice.
- Who are the drunken lost souls begging for your attention?
- Who are the lost children who want you to notice them?
- What might they be trying to say?
- What words or phrases keep repeating?

Write down your thoughts and ideas in your *Leap Journal*.

Prompt ~ I Don't Care ☑

Writing Exercise
Tools: Your *Leap Journal*, pen, and a timer
Time: Approximately 10 minutes + one week

Something powerful happens when we let go of needing to be perfect or needing to be seen in a certain way. In my own experience, being willing to take leaps imperfectly often leads our lives in exciting new directions; it works like magic.

Set a timer for 10 minutes.

Ask yourself:

- What would you love to do if you didn't care if you did it well or not?
- Make a list. Keep moving your pen or pencil until the timer goes off.

Which of your ideas sounds the most fun? Circle them. What is one you can do this week? Try it out and see what happens.

> *"Be at peace and see a clear pattern and plan running through all your lives. Nothing is by chance."*
>
> *~Eileen Caddy*

Second Chances

Reach up for an idea and
it is gone.

Where do they go?

Reach up to the clouds
to pull them down

They so like to escape up there.

Cast up a cord to capture.

Ground them.
Anchor them.

Beg them:
Stay just a while longer.

And if they get away,
don't give up.

Keep watch.

They will return
in different costumes

Flitting back
in their own sweet time.

Prompt ~ Cast a Cord ☑

Writing Exercise
Tools: Your *Leap Journal*, a pen, and a timer
Time: Approximately 10 minutes

Creative fragments often appear to us in our dreams, or during rote tasks like driving or taking a shower. For this prompt, we are going to create space for any wisps of inspiration trying to get our attention. Keep your pen moving. Write down anything that comes to you without questioning it or trying to change it.

Complete the following sentence in your *Leap Journal*:

- An idea that keeps flitting away from me is...

Imagine your idea or creative fragment is a character, or an entity with its own personality and voice. Have a conversation with this idea to see what else it has to say. For this prompt, use your dominant hand (right if right-handed) to ask the questions, and your non-dominant hand (left if right-handed, right if left-handed) to answer.

- Dominant hand, write: *Hello, idea. What do you want from me?*

- Non-dominant hand: *I want.... (Keep your pen moving.)*

- Dominant hand, write: *Hello idea. If I were to make more space for you in my life, what would you want to say?*

- Non-dominant hand: *I want to say.... (Write whatever comes.)*

When you are done, read what you have written. What is a simple way you can explore this idea or creative fragment more?

"...those little people, my brownies, who do one half of my work for me while I am half asleep, and in all human likelihood do the rest for me as well, when I am wide awake and fondly suppose I do it for myself."

~Robert Louis Stevenson

Inspiration

I noticed the breeze
on the small window
of my phone

Blowing through her window
at the same moment
it blew through mine
in the car where I was sitting,
window down

One puff of air
blowing in two places at once.

I think inspiration is like that,
weaving through the world
for anyone who will
catch it like a breeze
and write it down.

Prompt ~ Two Places at Once ☑

Research Activity
Tools: Your *Leap Journal*, a pen, timer, and the Internet
Time: Approximately one hour

We often hear of two researchers on opposite sides of the world coming up with similar theories or conclusions without knowing what the other was up to. Similarly, my closest friends and I often marvel at how we tend to go through similar personal growth experiences or have similar insights at the same time, even if we haven't talked in many months.

The more aligned we become with our own intuition and flow of creative ideas, the more we seem to energetically connect with others on similar paths, without even realizing it.

What if we were more intentional in how we access these energetic connections? In your *Leap Journal*, answer the following questions:

- Creative themes I am working with right now include...
- I keep thinking about...
- I am curious about...
- I am inspired about...
- Other thinkers, professionals, or creators who also seem passionate about these ideas include...
- A unique perspective I have to offer to the greater story that is unfolding includes...

Going Deeper

Spend about one hour researching a topic that you are passionate about. Write down key insights about what you discover in your *Leap Journal* or in a computer file. Remember to give credit to those whose ideas inspire you.

- What is a next step you can take to connect with people with similar ideas? How could you add your unique perspective to the conversation?

> "*I looked deeply into her eyes and realized that she, the universe, was me.*"
>
> *~Brené Brown*

Creative Vomit

It's like I am possessed with words,
they just keep coming.

"There, there"
I need someone to say,
to hold my shoulders
and support me
as I get everything out

Like a loved one does,
holding back our hair
from the bowl
when we are puking our brains out.

"Just get it out!"
we say as we purge
our insides turning outward

Until the creative vomiting stops.

And when it's done
and we get our wits about us
once more:

Clean up.
Wipe down.

Fold up
the crumbled papers,
splattered ink.

Close up shop.
Move on.

Empty now,
we start to fill up
on life
slowly again,
one bite at a time

Until we are too full
of the beauty
and pain
of this world
to bear it anymore
alone

And the
creative purge
starts up
all over again.

Prompt ~ Creative Purge ☀

Art Project (or other hobby)
Tools: Supplies related to a hobby you've been wanting to try, and a timer
Time: Approximately 10 minutes

Choose a creative project or hobby you've been wanting to try, or that you used to love to do, such as sketching, painting, or playing a musical instrument. The goal of this exercise is to get your creativity flowing as quickly as possible. Don't censor or judge. Let whatever comes to you flow, without making it right or wrong. This is a great way to connect with the energy of your inner creator, or True Self.

- Set out your supplies.
- Set a timer for 10 minutes.
- For the entire 10 minutes, do your chose "new" thing.
- Stay focused on how you feel rather than the outcome or quality of the product you are creating.
- If you ever feel stuck, just keep moving (energy flows where our attention goes).
- When your timer goes off, look at what you've made.
- Do you have any new realizations, ideas, or insights?
- What did it feel like to really get your energy moving in a creative way?
- How does it feel to have gotten all of that out of you?

> *"Life is a big canvas, throw all the paint on it you can."*
>
> *Danny Kaye*

My Muse

Live with me,
she beckons.
I can almost see
her skirt
twirling around her,
bare feet,
sandals in her hands.

Dance with me,
she says,
flitting across
the green fields
miles ahead of me,
or so it seems,
beseeching me to follow.

Twirl with me,
she says,
long white dress
shining like the
moonlight
against inky black sky.

Fall with me,
she says,
dropping, open arms
into white sand,
sinking like chocolate
into marshmallows
as if
it's exactly
what she must do.

Die with me,
she whispers,
pale as the night
after an especially
hard day,
pale skin
faint at the sight
of hardness.

"No, I say,
Come back!"
With my breath,
I whisper in reply.

She comes back
to full life again,
dancing,
playing,
laughing,
flying.

She is my Muse,
she and I,
Twin Sisters
from the
same mother,
born of
Creativity.

Prompt ~ Meet Your True Self ☀

Meditation + Art Project
Tools: Your *Leap Journal*, a pen, magic makers, and colored pencils
Time: Approximately 20 minutes

A powerful strategy for really getting our lives to flow and staying inspired is imagining our True Self or Muse as a character or actual entity with whom we can directly communicate. The key part of this process is to not take it too seriously. It's important to have fun, and remember that in our imaginations, anything is possible.

Each time you do this prompt, you might come up with something different. If nothing comes to you, simply make something up!

- Close your eyes.

- Pretend you are looking at a giant movie screen.

- Imagine your True Self appears on this screen.

- See who shows up. (Have fun with this!) It might be a man, woman, animal, spirit, angel, light, symbol, voice, etc. There is no right or wrong. If you don't see anything, then use your imagination and make up something. What could your True Self be like if you were to know?

- Another way to do this is to imagine entering the movie screen and embodying your True Self. Feel yourself *as* your True Self. What does it feel like to be energetically one with your True Self? Make any adjustments to your True Self's identity and energy. When you have fully experienced the deep peace that often comes when we are fully aligned with our True Self energy, in whatever way feels right to you, open your eyes.

- Sketch your imagined version of your True Self in your *Leap Journal*. Let your imagination run wild. The quality of your art doesn't matter. Stick figures are fine! You might see your True Self identity as a character, or simply as an energy or color. It's all okay.

- Next to your drawing, write some words that describe your True Self, or what it felt like to fully embody who you really are. What is your True Self's personality? What do you act like when you fully embody your True Self? What is your true vibe?

- What is a name that feels right for this version of you, your True Self? If you don't know, guess. Write it down in your *Leap Journal*.

Prompt ~ True Self Meditation ♥

Meditation
Tools: A quiet, private place and yourself, your *Leap Journal*, and a pen
Time: Approximately 20 minutes

Now that you've imagined your True Self, let's go one step further and get to know them in a deeper way.

- Take a few nice, deep breaths.
- Do whatever you need to feel safe and to deeply relax.
- Close your eyes.
- Imagine going to a safe space where you are completely protected.
- When you are ready, invite your True Self to join you there in this safe space.
- Imagine having a conversation with your True Self as if they are a real person, sitting there beside you like an imaginary friend.
- What message does your True Self offer you?
- Now imagine your True Self gives you a big hug and the two of you merge, becoming one.

Write down any insights in your *Leap Journal*.

> *"I learned that the real creator was my inner Self, the Shakti…that desire to do something is God inside talking through us."*
>
> *Michele Shea*

My Writing

My writing has become my comfort,
that blanket one wraps up in
tight and cozy,
perfectly tucked,
where all is right,
where one could sleep
motionless
all night.

My writing has become
my second mother,
the ultimate parent,
who speaks the words
we most need to hear
in times of trouble
and tells us the harsh truth
when we have deluded
even ourselves.

My writing has become
my lover,
the one who whispers
of our loveliness
even when we feel none at all,
almost lifeless,
in need of revival,
and then,
with the in-breath
we become full again.

My writing has become
my foundation,
that firm touchstone
we swim to at the bottom of a lake,
feeling our way through darkness
until our toes squish,
something to push against,
to rise up to the
masked light above.

My writing has become
my salvation and
my friend,
my mirror and my magnet,
my attraction to what's next,
the torch guiding me through
the darkest of caves,
drawing me out
like a firefly draws out the child
from the screened-in porch
to wander barefoot
amongst the day's last treasures.

My writing has become
my message
my memory
my motion
my blood and my breath,
pulsing through everything I do
and everything I am,
reconnecting me to life itself,
reminding me of
the very reason I am here.

Prompt ~ Love Letter to Your Hobby ♥

Writing Exercise
Tools: Your *Leap Journal* and a pen
Time: Approximately 20 minutes

We often say that we *love* certain activities, such as arranging flowers, gardening, writing, painting, and dancing. For this prompt, we are going to take that love and run with it. This prompt can help us deepen our commitment to doing what brings us joy.

Using your *Leap Journal*, write a love letter to your hobby or an activity that inspires you. Include your answers to the below questions.

You might begin your letter: Beloved ____ (insert name of hobby, activity, such as writing, musical, or meditation practice, etc.)

- I love you because…
- I yearn for us, together, to…
- I look forward to when….
- I promise to…
- Thank you for…

> *"An artist is like a lover who cannot pause to entertain the possibility of being spurned. He must press his suit. His whole impulse is to love."*
>
> *~Julia Cameron*

The Visitor

I am so grateful
that it's happened today
in this way

This Voice,
coming to me,
flowing at me.

I wonder,
"When will it stop?"

As if it's a chapter book
I've just picked up,
and at some point
will finish.

I wonder these things
as the words
flow through me.

"Will it ever stop?"

I hope not.

For, each word,
flowing through my brain
cleanses me somehow,
makes me new.

No matter
whether it does or
does not,
for,
because
it is here now,
this Visitor,
the Poet,

I will forever
be changed.

Prompt ~ Your Creative Voice ☀

Meditation
Tools: A quiet, private place, your *Leap Journal,* and a pen
Time: Approximately 20 minutes

Think of an issue that has been bothering you, or some area of your life where you could use some support or reassurance. We often think the answer lies *out there*. However, sometimes tapping our own inner peace is far more effective.

- Close your eyes and sit quietly.

- Imagine a loving, completely accepting, kind voice is talking to you, offering love, comfort, reassurance, and acceptance.

- Listen quietly to whatever comes as if it is from another source, from some place outside of you. Try to be present and aware.

- It might help to pay attention to the air around the crown of your head. It can also be helpful to pay special attention to the ground beneath your feet or the way it feels to be sitting on your chair, to help you feel grounded.

- Pay attention to anything you hear or feel, the way you would to a loved one telling you something important. If you have trouble with this, then simply imagine what advice or words of wisdom your True Self might offer the other parts of you.

- If at any point you feel uncomfortable while doing this exercise, take a break and start again. If you don't like the voice or message that comes, simply ask for another one, one that is completely loving and knows what is in your best interest.

- When you've finished your conversation, imagine surrounding your body with a healing, loving, clearing golden or white light.

Write down any new intuitive insights you've received in your *Leap Journal*.

"Learn to get in touch with the silence within yourself and know that everything in this life has a purpose."

~Elisabeth Kubler-Ross

Self-Reflection

~Staying Inspired~

Living in a state of inspiration is like a game—taking little leaps toward things, people, and environments that make us feel good, hopeful, uplifted, and engaged, and little leaps away from those that drain our energy, bore, or make us doubt ourselves, our intuition, or what is possible. Here are a few more questions to help you fine-tune your own unique formula for staying inspired.

- What does "feeling inspired" mean to you?
- How do you act when you are inspired?
- What environments make you feel most inspired?
- What types of people inspire you?
- Who are some authors, artists, or musicians who inspire you?
- Whom do you love to be around? Who uplifts you?
- What kind of activities fill you with joy?

What's Your Leap?

What's a simple change you can make in your life to feel more inspired?

Process

What works for *you*?

Most mornings, I wake up, put on my slippers, and shuffle out to the kitchen before the rest of my family. I feel my way through the darkness, hit the start button on the coffee pot, listening for the gurgling to start and the glow of the little red light.

Then I plop down on the couch, pull my favorite furry blanket over my still sleepy body, grab my binder filled with clean, unlined paper and write whatever comes to my mind. Without writing like this, first thing in the morning, I feel a bit lost, out of sorts. It's like drinking the coffee, something I must do, a rhythm I must keep or else I'll get a headache.

For me, writing is like clearing out all my thoughts that gathered overnight, meeting myself again, there on the empty page and rediscovering who and how I am, today. When I don't do this, I'm off. I wander about not knowing quite what to do next. I roam, searching, like a dog unsettled when his owner was expected but is not yet home.

I used to think my desire to be a writer was about seeing my name on a book cover, being received by others. That was when I was doing it in fits and starts, before I was doing it every day. Now that I write every day, I know better. The truth is, being a writer is about being who I am, nothing more or less.

For me, it's not so much about inventing something new, it's more about discovering and uncovering something. It's about letting a story, essay, or poem unfold simply because we are at last together—ideas, pen, paper. We are finally finding each other in one place, time cleared on the calendar for our sacred meeting. For me, writing is like being a witness to words that are partly from me, partly about me. Words heal my deepest crevices once and for all, sewing them shut in a way that finally makes sense.

Whether it's a hobby we love, other people's art or music that we enjoy, or simply being in a beautiful place in nature, I believe there are many activities that can help do this for us, that awaken that inner spark that makes us feel more alive. In this state of flow and openness to whatever is happening within us and around us, I believe we send out a little bit of light, a reminder to others that life is good, and that this joy is available also to them.

For me, as a writer, the ability to make sense of my deepest thoughts and see connections, to use them to then create something that can later be absorbed and consumed is almost like a game. Perhaps it's the way an archeologist feels when she discovers an unexpected treasure, brushing off crumbs gently, watching as the relic reveals itself.

Museumgoers later look through glass, separate from the treasure. But the explorer always has the connection she and the relic shared when it first emerged from the rubble. The sacred feeling of lifting something up from the underground to be witnessed by others and shared is the real gift. For the one who helps inspiration find its form, that thing there on the shelf of the museum or library must be nothing short of magic.

Support on our journeys often comes from friends who know the joy of being in synch with their True Selves - whether through making the perfect basketball shot, feeling the joy of being completely present with another during a heartfelt conversation, or knowing the feeling of hitting the perfect note with which to finish their own song. Each of these acts is about the magic of discovering, uncovering, and unearthing what already exists, but has simply lay hidden away, forgotten.

I think connecting with our inner voice and following where it leads us is the ultimate rebellion; we tap our inner teenager, our want-to-leave-the-pack-to-find-ourselves energy, determined to discover the best way to lift our inner voice, our sacred energy within up from the rubble without too much damage.

As a writer, for me, editing is the dusting off, making sure this thing—this unrepeatable gift that had lain waiting all this time—is now ready for others to pry, poke, prod, and witness too. Editing is like showing up to be with a favorite friend on the train platform as she prepares to leave us, maybe forever. We want to get in that last big hug before she goes off on her way.

When it comes to our own process of uncovering and creating, no matter what form it takes, we each have our own strategies that work best for us. Figuring them out is what turns our medicine into magic. We can't be told how to turn our lives into art; we must toil our way into answers.

Over time we learn that right for them doesn't have to be right for us; at some point we all need to emerge, allowing our own unique truth and worth to be revealed. Some of us wear lucky hats, some fast, some binge, some nibble chocolate and popcorn throughout our own process of tuning in. Some of us wake early. Some of us go to sleep late. Some of us sneak out in the middle of the night, flirting with both wakefulness and sleep, finding that being smack dab in the middle of the veil feeds our magic.

Some of us commune with our Muse like our Maker, others grip hard to sharpened pencils on carefully cleared desks with legal pads and index cards, cursing our way through every word or brush stroke as we write, solve, invent, paint, and create. No method is right, no pathway wrong. Some create invisibly while sitting in meditation or consume others' art like a box of decadent chocolates. The key is figuring out what works for each of us in each unique moment of our lives.

There is a reason, I believe, why the most famous spiritual stories include dark nights of the soul—40 days and 40 nights. Wise sages have modeled what we all at some point in our lives come to know; miracles happen through face-to-face encounters with own humanity.

Dark nights offer instruction and a reminder. Each of us must oversee our own unique process for allowing the True Self to step forward and take its rightful place at the helm of our lives. When we are willing to stay with ourselves through the unearthing of truths and our own sufferings, our capacity to hear the profound wisdom that no one can teach us expands.

How we do our thing, how we tap into a voice chatting away within is personal and important, possibly the most important thing we will ever do. Our intuitive, creative process is as much a work of art as what we ultimately produce, although it may never be known by another.

The process by which we live our lives is where the real work gets done—where the healing happens, the tearing down, throwing out, getting out of our own way, getting rid of our demons, and ushering aside those versions of self that have gotten in our way—allowing us to reunite again and again with our own True Selves.

Process is how we learn to handle those voices haunting and taunting, telling us there is not enough time, we've been doing it all wrong, or whatever form self-doubt, or inner or outer demons take for each of us. The moments where we turn away from all of that and face the truth that we are different from any other person in the entire world, and that our process is personal and private, rare, and unrepeatable is when we step into the delicate process of sharing our unique sparks with the world.

"I don't accept the judging of process. We're all trying to get to the same island. Whether you swim, fly, surf, or skydive in, it doesn't matter. What matters is when the red light comes on."

~Jerry Seinfeld

Still A Writer

On those days
when you
sit
on hard chair

Staring at the
blank page
or
computer screen
with cursor
blinking back

You are still a writer.

Prompt ~ Still You ☑

Research Activity
Tools: A quiet, private place, your *Leap Journal,* and a pen
Time: Approximately 20 minutes

Have you ever had one of those days (or weeks, months, or years) where you felt stuck, or as if you were no longer living life as the positive, inspired, intuitive person that you are?

Still You

Write in your *Leap Journal* about a time in your life when you felt stuck.

- How did that downturn affect your perspective or feelings of self-worth?

- What helped?

- What didn't?

- How did you ultimately get through this experience?

- What new perspectives did you gain about your own self-identity or self-worth, for better or worse? What choices did you make?

Option: Still Them

Another way to do this prompt is to think of someone you know who went through a downturn but has since had a turnaround. You can choose someone from your own personal circle, or a well-known figure such as an actor, artist, musician, creator, writer, or athlete.

- How did they ultimately get through their challenge?
- What helped?
- What didn't?
- What new perspectives do you think they gained, for better or worse? (If you're not sure, ask them, or take your best guess.)

Compare your story to theirs.

- What do both stories have in common?
- What, if any, were the differences between the two stories?
- What lessons were gained?
- Did you gain any insights that might apply to your life?
- Which turnaround formula worked best?

> *"When we are no longer able to change a situation, we are challenged to change ourselves."*
>
> *~Viktor Frankl*

Why I Wake Up

I wake up
To write madly
To access the vein
To steep the tea
To mull the brew
To catch the words
before the rest of the world is
talking too loudly for me to hear.

Prompt ~ Access the Vein ☑

Writing Exercise + Mindfulness Activity
Tools: Your *Leap Journal* and a pen
Time: One week

We each have our own formula for hearing our intuition, boosting our creativity, and changing our lives for the better. The key is figuring it out. For one week, pay attention to when your life is flowing and when it's not, and what choices made the difference.

Notice where and when you get intuitive hits, when you feel closest to your own True Self, and when you feel most creative. What gets in your way of hearing your own inner voice? What helps you access your intuitive and creative vein?

Take notes in your *Leap Journal*.

- What changes could you make in your own life to feel more connected to your True Self, and more confident about taking creative leaps?
- What helps your life flow?

> *"Those who flow as life flows know they need no other force."*
>
> ~Lao Tzu

Mornings

No interaction with others
That's the rule
For interacting with oneself.

No eye contact
Except with thine own

Crouching in a cave
And from that quiet hovel
Watching the world go by.

I listen and hear
Nothing

But sounds of my soul.

This is the way to start a day.

Prompt ~ Start a Day ☑

Life Practice
Tools: Your *Leap Journal*, a pen, calendar, and tools for your new routine
Time: One week

The expression that it's important to make a good first impression can be true in many contexts. How we start something often has a great impact its overall journey. This can be true in relationships, projects, and in each day.

Answer the following questions in your *Leap Journal*:

- How does your regular morning routine reflect who you really are, and what is most important to you?
- What's working?
- What's not?
- What are some new steps you might want to add?
- What's something you want to eliminate or change?
- What would you like your new morning routine to be?
- What kind of support systems might help make your new morning routine a success?

Practice your new morning routine for one week, checking each day off in your calendar when you do. At the end of the week, assess:

- What changes, if any, did you notice in your energy, synchronicities, creativity, or intuitive insights?

- What worked?
- What didn't?
- What might make your new routine even more aligned with who you really are, and where you want your life to go?

The important thing about this prompt is to remember that we don't have to wait for tomorrow morning to reset. Once we learn what works for us, each moment becomes an opportunity to restart our day and begin again.

> *"You didn't think when you got up this morning that this would be the day your life would change, did you? But it's going to happen because the only thing that stands between you and grand success in living are these two things: Getting started and never quitting!"*
>
> ~Robert Schuller

The Secret

I feel as if I just discovered

The Secret

To making life work
to Sanity
to Sanctity
to Discovery
to Peace.

It's all about waking early

And on occasion, making it to a beach,
or at least to pen and paper

Before the rest of the world knows
it's a new day.

Who knew it could be so easy?

Prompt ~ What's Your Secret? ☑

Writing Exercise
Tools: Your *Leap Journal* and a pen
Time: 10 minutes

Have you ever felt as if you've discovered a secret to feeling more productive, energetic, or inspired? How about healthier? Have you tried a new habit, new diet, or exercise program that made you really felt great? How about a secret to hearing your intuition or inner voice?

- What is your personal good-energy secret?
- How well are you implementing what you know works best for you in your own life?
- What changes could you make to better nurture your creativity, your relationship with your intuition, or a positive outlook?

Make a list of all the things you know work for you in your *Leap Journal*.

> *"Let yourself be silently drawn by the strange pulling of what you really love. It will not lead you astray."*
>
> *Rumi*

Finding Gold

Why is it
that I only hear
one bird,
one long melodious tone
against the backdrop
of so many?

Why is it
that I hear
traffic humming,
zeroing in on
that truck
on the freeway
jumbling along
with a clang
instead of
the symphony of crickets?

How is it
that we choose
what to focus on,
one trouble,
one piece of bad news
against children's handprints,
playful sounds
asking for our attention too
so we can remember
how good life can be?

Clamoring all of it,
like we,
to be seen.

Choose me!

It doesn't matter if it's good for us
or if it resonates
with our own rare tune.

We just notice
whatever it is that we will.

Blue skies
or pure white ones

Sunshine
or clouds

Mist hovering,
zooming in

Dog barking

Crow crowding out
the tiny silver tingling
of a finch
calling mother from a nest
for food

How do we make sense
of it all,
so much noise
and beauty
and pain
invoked from life,
the simple fact of birth,
all of it crowded in
accidentally
together?

How do we sift
through it
like a beachcomber
for whom a shell
is not good enough,
taking out, instead,
a large metal sieve
and tossing sand,
grain by grain
through it

Until she finds

Gold.

Prompt ~ Finding Gold ☀

Mindfulness Activity
Tools: You!
Time: 3 minutes

Getting our lives to flow is all about bringing how we live into attunement and alignment with who we *really* are in each moment. Appreciating and being aware of what is happening outside of ourselves as well as inside is a powerful process for expanding our hearts and our creativity.

- Take a deep breath.

- Notice how the air feels as it goes through your nose and fills your lungs.

- What are you smelling in this moment?

- How does the air around your body feel? Move your body. How does your body feel? What feels good? What doesn't?

- How do you feel in relation to your environment?

- Close your eyes. Pay attention to what you hear. What sounds, if any, jump out to be noticed?

- What do you love about this moment? What catches your attention? What do you appreciate?

- What else do you notice? What hadn't you noticed before doing this exercise?

Prompt ~ Choose Me! ☀

Art Project
Tools: You!
Time: 10 minutes

Notice something in your current environment that catches your attention like a smell, beautiful object, sound, etc.

- Find a way to honor this object through art. You could draw it, paint a picture of it, or take a photo of it.

- Try to express what makes this object so special as if you were describing it to someone from another universe or who has never experienced anything like it.

Prompt ~ Love It All ☀

Writing Exercise
Tools: Your *Leap Journal* and a pen
Time: 10 minutes

Choose an object and write a love letter to it, mentioning everything that makes it so special. You might choose the item from the previous prompt, the *Finding Gold* meditation, something you dislike, or something you love.

Another way to do this prompt is to write the love letter to *you*.

After you have completed this exercise, take a few minutes to reflect on what it felt like to be the witness, and to have the rare job of appreciating this beautiful object (or yourself) from a place of gratitude and deep appreciation.

- How do you *feel*?
- What unique perspective did you offer?

Write your insights in your *Leap Journal*.

> *"The universe buries strange jewels deep within us all, and then stands back to see if we can find them."*
>
> ~*Elizabeth Gilbert*

I Gave In

I gave in,
knowing it was going to
keep happening
and
kept my pen and paper
by my nightstand.

I relinquished
my tight hold
on scheduled writing sessions
and accepted
that the words were going to
keep tumbling down

whenever they
damn well chose.

Prompt ~ Capturing Ideas ☑

Writing Exercise + Life Practice
Tools: Your *Leap Journal*, a pen, and any other tools needed for your ideas
Time: 10 minutes + one week

Sometimes, when life gets busy, it can be difficult to find time to capture our creative ideas and intuitive hits. The purpose of this exercise is to brainstorm practical new ways that work for *you*.

Complete these sentences in your *Leap Journal*. Write down everything that comes to mind.

- I get most of my creative ideas when...
- I often get a sense of what to do next when...
- Some of my best ideas come when...
- For me, the best way to catch ideas is...
- It rarely works when I...
- I'm curious if this will work...
- I know this helps...

Challenge yourself to come up with as many ways for capturing your creative ideas as you can. Examples might include keeping a notepad by your bedside or in your bathroom so you can jot down ideas you get in the middle of the night, or after taking a shower.

Or you might want to experiment with sending yourself emails using the audio function on your phone (something that a fellow author taught me!). Write down all your ideas in your *Leap Journal.*

Choose your favorite ideas to experiment with for one week.

- Make a list of supplies you need to implement the ideas. For example, do you need to buy a box of pens and extra notebooks? Do you need to download an application on your phone?

> "*Each of us is an artist, capable of conceiving and creating a vision from the depths of our being.*"
>
> ~*Dorothy Fadiman*

You'll Need It Someday

Don't think
that school writing
doesn't matter,
I say in response to
a child's
studious rebellion.

Tasks like this,
footnotes and research,
checking others' words
so annoyingly tedious
are like churning butter.

They prime the pump,
grease the wheel,
make sure the battery is charged

And remind you
that you have a voice.

Because you'll need it someday.

Prompt ~ Annoyingly Tedious ☑

Writing Exercise + Life Practice
Tools: Daily life, your *Leap Journal*, and a pen
Time: One week

Think of an area of your life where you are faced with annoyingly tedious tasks. Examples might include how a musician might feel about playing scales, a writer might feel about proofreading, a chef might feel about washing dishes, or an artist might feel about cleaning her paintbrushes. Complete the following sentences in your *Leap Journal*:

- My annoying activity is…
- When I do this activity, this happens…
- When I don't do this activity, this happens…
- If I were to do this activity more often, I would…
- If I weren't to do this activity ever again, I would…
- Another way I can accomplish the same thing would be…
- This activity would be a lot more fun if…

Choose one change to how you approach this activity based on your responses. Examples might include getting help, doing your activity with others in community, playing music while doing it, setting an artificial deadline so you do the task more quickly, etc. Record what happens. Fine-tune your approach as needed.

> *"It's not that I'm so smart, it's just that I stay with problems longer."*
>
> ~Albert Einstein

Busy

I have been working.

But no one knows it.

I've taken to
writing down
just one line
at a time.

It's all I can do
to keep up.

Prompt ~ One Joy at a Time ☑

Mindfulness Activity
Tools: Anything required for a favorite activity
Time: Five minutes

When our lives are busy, it is natural to think we don't have time to do something that brings us joy or a new habit that might be good for us. This exercise is about retraining our brains to experience joy and presence in small spurts.

What is an activity that brings you joy? Doodling? Dancing? Sitting in the sunlight? Reading? Playing music?

- Set a timer for five minutes and spend the entire five minutes completely focused on this uplifting, joyful activity.

If you can't think of an activity, or still don't think you have enough time, try this:

- Write one line that sums up how you are feeling in this moment. Try to keep it under 20 words.

Whatever happens each time you do this prompt, just let it be. After you are done, notice how you feel.

> *"Great things are not done by impulse, but by a series of small things brought together."*
>
> *~Vincent Van Gogh*

Choose Wisely

I would rather choose wisely
which word for which purpose.

Creation is
so much more interesting
than butchery.

Cutting things up,
then wiping down
the chopping floor.

No, I would rather just
choose wisely.

Prompt ~ Choose Wisely ☑

Meditation + Writing Activity
Tools: Your *Leap Journal* and a pen
Time: 20 minutes

Sometimes we follow other people's footsteps or do what our friends, coworkers, or families expect or want from us, rather than taking the time to tune inward and make conscious choices about what we want, or where our intuition is guiding us to go.

Often the answer isn't doing more, it's letting go. Think of a project you are currently working on or want to begin. This can be something related to your creativity, business, hobby, or any project on your to-do list right now.

- Take a deep breath.
- Close your eyes.
- Imagine your desired outcome.
- What would be a dream-come-true for you and this idea?
- How might you feel when your dream has come true?
- What would you need to let go of for your desired outcome to happen?
- Take another deep breath.

After doing this meditation, answer the following questions in your *Leap Journal*:

- To experience your dream as you imagined, what is something you need to say *No* to?
- What is something you need to say *Yes* to?

> *"Listen to your own voice, your own soul. Too many people listen to the noise of the world, instead of themselves."*
>
> ~Leon Brown

Remembering to Forget

My children laugh
as I can't find my glasses

Like the tune
of an old woman
I thought I'd never sing.

Is it aging?
I wonder.

But then I know it's not.
It has always been like this.

"Are you writing?"
a friend asks.

I cock my head for a moment, contemplating.
Why yes, I believe I am.

Times like these
when I can't get to pen and paper
and the voice prattles on and on
are why I missed
that appointment

Or wandered about
with a dazed look
walking aimlessly
around
that parking garage
looking for my car.

Only true friends
know my struggle
and how to put everything right

With loving words like
"You're just a deep thinker"

Or better yet,
helping me find what I've lost.

And so, while it might not
be mindful,
and monks
might turn their noses up
at my mind wandering
until lovingkindness
turns them back down into a bow

I still don't know if I would trade
my mind wandering and forgetfulness
for Being Here Now
always.

Because,
while there is much to be said
for being in one's body
and
taking a deep breath
and
noticing the
colors
of a
bright bug
against
rough brick
or hearing
the birds sing
as if
only
for
you
or yes,
even feeling
your own pain
as it
cuts like a knife
through your heart
(because that is mindful too),
sometimes
I love to get lost
in the
world of words
that drop down
from above
into my consciousness
if only I can retain them
long enough
to find a pen.

So now,
you are among the few
who know
the Truth.

Now you understand too
the real reason
why I
so often
remember to forget.

Prompt ~ Remember to Forget ☑

Writing Exercise
Tools: Your *Leap Journal* and a pen
Time: 10 minutes

Make a list of all the things that might slip through the cracks if you were to live the life of your dreams, follow your passions, or get deep into a creative project calling to you.

In an ideal scenario, what distractions would you love to let go of so that you could devote as much time as you wanted to follow where your inner voice is calling you to go?

Complete the following sentences:

- Something I'd love to forget is...
- Something that keeps me from remembering is...
- Something I'd rather be doing is...

"We are fragile creatures, expected to function at high rates of speed, and asked to accomplish great and small things each day...The way to accomplish the assignment of truly living is to engage fully, richly, and deeply in the living of your dreams."

~S.A.R.K

Picking Up the Pen

We shouldn't think
we have no part
in our creations.

Opening the notebook

Picking up the pen

Paying attention

These count for something.

Prompt ~ Small Steps Count ☑

Writing Exercise
Tools: Your *Leap Journal* and a pen
Time: 20 minutes

Think of an activity that brings you joy and gets you in a state of flow—that zone where we are so engaged in what we are doing that we often lose track of time.

- What is something simple that would enable you to experience this state more often?

Examples might include organizing or finding your art supplies, buying a how-to book, tuning your musical instrument, clearing time on your calendar, or pulling out a pen and paper and writing a quick three-line poem, etc.

- Are there any little details of your life that you can let go of or delegate so that you can do this activity more often?

Write your ideas down.

> *"Now you begin again, your life an untwisting of continual beginnings – the way a spider plant, whose roots have outgrown the pot, releases a cascade of offspring, all those green legs reaching for the ground."*
>
> *~Emily Ruth Hazel*

Self-Reflection

~Honoring Your Own Process~

We are often taught that there is a certain way of doing things, or that experts know best. When we put too much stock into other people's advice, we can start to doubt our innate wisdom. Leaping is all about trusting ourselves. Here are a few more questions to help you identify the creative processes that work best for you when it comes to getting your life to flow.

- What's working in your life? What's not?

- What would your ideal, most-productive day be like?

- What's your lucky hat? In other words, do you have a favorite trick or way of doing your best work? What helps you to be more productive? What boosts your creativity? What boosts your intuition? What positively affects the quality of your work?

- What rules do you have for your life? Which are most helpful? Which are no longer helpful or would you like to change?

- Imagine you had to train someone else in how you live your best life. What is your unique formula? Create a *Creative User's Manual* outlining all the steps they'd need to take, and all your tips and tricks for living life as *you*.

What's Your Leap?

What's a simple change you can make that would improve how well your life flows?

Blocks

What's in your way?

I was talking with a friend about how difficult it can be to put something out into the world that is unedited and imperfect. Both of us are recovering over-achievers and perfectionists, sometimes less in recovery than we would like. Perhaps you're like us. Maybe you sometimes fall for the cultural mantra that the more we do, produce, or create, and the higher quality our creations, the more valuable we are. Maybe you too know what it feels like to care what others think or to want to be seen in a certain way.

When we spend too much time looking outward, focused more on what we are achieving than how we feel, or when we fall into the trap of seeking others' approval, life's flow often gets stuck. We may freeze, afraid to make a mistake, or be so gripped with anxiety about being misjudged or misunderstood that we don't allow ourselves to trust our innate creativity and follow where it wants to take us.

When our lives feel blocked or stuck, for whatever reason, we are almost always coming up against something from outside of our True Selves, often from our past, whether past emotional patterns, habits, beliefs about who we are that were passed down to us, conclusions about our abilities that we reached when we were very young, or traumatic experiences that we haven't yet healed or integrated. All of these can lodge in our self-perceptions and block not just our creativity but also the greater flow of our lives.

Even if we intuitively know our blocks aren't who we really are—old debris or coping mechanisms—we may resist doing anything about them because they are so familiar and make us feel safe. Other times, even when we want to change, we might not know where to turn for support, or might not yet realize there is another way.

Sometimes we may even unconsciously believe that our blocks are protecting us or not realize that they might be the very thing holding us back from letting go and leaping into a new reality. Regardless of how difficult our past has been, or how stuck we feel, the quiet, loving, creative voice within us is always there. Whether we choose to listen and what we do about it, however, is up to us.

I like to look at creative flow as coming from a higher source, since that's so often how it feels. Somewhere upstream, a creative energy trickles drop by drop, yearning to find its way through our blocks. As it gathers strength and momentum, it can take more and more effort to block the flow of the rushing energy that wants us to experience firsthand who we really are, and our lives to feel joyful and full. When, for any reason, we weaken our resistance against life's natural flow, slowly, a trickle starts to get through; drop by drop, drip by drip, and our creativity often starts to awaken in unexpected ways.

We are constantly evolving and changing. Flow happens when we start letting go of what is no longer real, true, or aligned with who we are in the present moment. When we are reconnecting with our own inner flow after a time of feeling disconnected, we might feel like we are letting go of all that is familiar and entering a new world. But really, we are only letting go of what was never us to make room for who we have always been, quenching our very basic thirst for our own True Selves.

Learning how to heal and release our creative and intuitive blocks, integrating all aspects of who we are, is not always easy. Even when we tell ourselves we are ready to take a leap, whatever that means for us, we may still clench our teeth, shuttering, shivering, telling ourselves it is all a mistake. We may feel scared to death to change habitual patterns that have protected us in the past. It can feel dangerous to rip off our facades, to be fully seen, come out of hiding, or say what has for so long has been left unsaid, chancing being maligned or misunderstood.

The first step is coming to know and accept ourselves in a deeper and fuller way. The second step is interacting in the world based on our own self-knowledge, showing this fuller version of who we really are to others. Knowing when it's time to share a fuller expression of ourselves with the outer world, or to share work we have created from the heart is delicate. We each have an innate wisdom about when our precious creations are ready to be birthed, when we are ready, and when it would be better to wait, heal, or integrate our own wisdom a little bit longer.

When we are birthing something new in our lives, the process is raw, precious, and fragile. We need to beware of overly helpful friends, loved ones, or well-intentioned-but-stuck fellow creatives or teachers who may prod and pry, encouraging us to share our work or our findings before we are ready. On the other hand, when the time is right and we don't take risks, or fully express ourselves in a way that is authentic, that can block our flow too, making us feel stagnant and stuck, preventing new ideas, new inspiration, and creations from taking form.

It's easy to get confused along the way. Often the right time isn't when our creative work is ready, our ideas are well thought out, we have outgrown our lives, or when others are ready for what we have to offer, but when *we* are—when we have also done the inner work needed to prepare ourselves for the change that ultimately always happens when we act in a way that is original and aligned with our truth. The key seems to be both not taking ourselves too seriously and treating the gifts we've received from a higher source with respect, no matter how minor, imperfect, or unimportant we may assume them to be.

After we've taken a leap and have shared ourselves more authentically, or released our unique creations, we reach yet another tricky point. Looking outward too long, living vicariously through others' reactions to something we have just shared can separate us again from creative flow. Turning outward always runs the risk of stopping our joyful, creative flow by focusing too much on how we are perceived instead of getting on with the business of tuning into where our inner voice wants to take us *next*. Whether our creative expressions cause others to look away in discomfort or awaken them to their own creative voice, triggering their own revolution from within is not our responsibility.

It's also important not to misunderstand silence or even criticism as meaning it wasn't the right time to make a change, or to share our truth or idea. If we don't win other people's approval, it's very often simply because we are trying to sell our wares to the wrong folks at the wrong moment. How we are perceived is a story about who is perceiving us, not about who we really are, or our value. Our job is to honestly share our message, release, integrate, and heal anything blocking us, then once again return to the important work of tapping our own inner voice.

Every great turning point, whether a quiet revelation or one that upturned a nation started first as an intuitive, creative nudge from within. Someone like us was courageous enough to demonstrate the unpopular idea that blocks, especially those put in our paths by others, are meant to be toppled.

When we challenge those limiting voices or patterns in our own brains that want our True Selves to stay hidden and silent, that's when real change happens. It is in wrestling with our blocks that we change our inner lives. It is in moving past our blocks and sharing what once seemed too fragile, too raw, vulnerable, or real that we change our outer lives. When we invite and support others in doing the same, we help change the world.

> *"The curious paradox is that when I accept myself just as I am, then I can change."*
>
> ~Carl Rogers

Rough Night

There now,
another rough night.

They happen.

We all know
how something gets stuck
and wakes us.

The next day,
we comfort ourselves,
jogging free
the cog in the wheel
so we can create again.

Prompt: Meet Your Ideal Parent ♥

Writing Exercise
Tools: Your *Leap Journal* and a pen
Time: 10 minutes

The key to moving through creative or intuitive blocks is to develop a strong, loving inner voice. When we do this, we gain direct access to our True Selves. As a result, emotional triggers and traumas slowly lose their grip because there is another energy supporting us even when our smaller selves feel vulnerable.

Imagine a perfect, ideal, completely loving and accepting parent is comforting you or offering loving encouragement regarding a challenge you are currently experiencing.

- What are some of the things this loving, ideal parent might say?
- What would be most helpful?
- What would help you to feel truly respected, valued, seen, and reassured?

Write a letter to yourself in the voice of this ideal, accepting, perfectly loving parent. This could be the start of a life-changing relationship.

Prompt: Ideal Parent Meditation 

Meditation
Tools: A quiet, private place
Time: 10 minutes

Our imaginations can be very powerful when it comes to accessing the power of our True Selves and getting our lives to flow.

- Close your eyes. Take a nice deep breath.
- Imagine a perfect, ideal, completely loving and accepting parent is with you.
- Spend some time with this completely loving being.
- See if they have any words of wisdom for you.
- Enjoy the experience of being loved unconditionally, just as you are.
- Whenever you feel complete, slowly begin to open your eyes.

> *"Peace of mind comes from not wanting to change others, but by simply accepting them as they are."*
>
> *~Gerald G. Jampolsky*

Stealing In the Night

If I didn't know
any better,
I would think
they were trying
to get away with something

Stealing
in the night.

Hiding.

Isn't that what we all do?

When we don't want to
face some truth?

Hiding from ourselves,
hiding behind the falsehoods,
grimaces and
fake smiles
that we so often
wear.

What if instead
we ripped them off like a
fairytale's costume
and looked
at the remnants
that lay beneath?

Unbidden treasures,
dreams
not yet begun
let alone acknowledged.

Griefs denied
hearts broken
too many times
to count
or to be pieced together.

Anger
bridling up
so scary
we hide and pretend
as if
that would protect us,
armor of denial.

What if we used
paper and pen
instead,
Creativity
as a weapon,
slicing our way
with ink marks and etchings
and found there
something more?

Something lost
beneath the rubble
of emotion,
too confusing.
too confining.
to see through.

What if there,
under the master of falsehoods,
we found
the glistening shimmering of our own Light
and this message:

You are enough
and it is all okay?

Prompt: Loving All of You 

Meditation
Tools: A quiet, private place
Time: 1-30 minutes

Sometimes our expectations for how we want ourselves or others to be don't leave enough space for the messiness and imperfections of life. Rather than inspiring us to stretch or reach new heights, unrealistic standards can cause us to bury, deny, or reject aspects of ourselves that we or others view as shameful, or that we wish didn't exist.

We might compare ourselves to others, not realizing that everyone has things about themselves that make them feel insecure. In fact, those people who appear to be the most put together or successful often have the most difficult relationships with those aspects of their personalities that are inconsistent with their mastery in other areas of their lives.

The more we reject aspects of ourselves, others, or truths, the more destructive these aspects often become, sometimes erupting in ways that cause harm. Avoiding what makes us feel uncomfortable can also make us feel separate from ourselves and our own humanity, and can make our imperfections feel worse than they are.

Welcoming it all in, accepting all of ourselves and others rather than rejecting those aspects that are unhealed or imperfect is a rare, powerful skill that often takes a lifetime to learn. Acceptance allows us to connect deeply with others rather than putting up more barriers. The more we can do this, the more we will experience shifts that help our lives to flow—sometimes in ways that are so dramatic they feel like miracles.

We learn acceptance through practice, by learning to stay with rather than run away from aspects of ourselves that we wish were different, and loving ourselves through whatever comes our way. For this prompt, think of one specific aspect of your personality or self that you often wish were different, or you often avoid, or for which, in the past, someone has judged you harshly.

If you ever feel stuck or if this meditation becomes too difficult, pause or get support. Every person on the face of the earth knows what it is like to feel insecure. It can take time to build up our acceptance muscles.

- Close your eyes.

- Take a few nice deep breaths.

- Focus on what about yourself you wish were different.

- Be curious about it. Witness it as if for the first time. What do you notice? Pay close attention to everything about it with an open mind. What might this part of your personality be trying to help you achieve?

- Imagine loving this aspect of self as if it were a young child, or helpless baby animal. Surround it with a radiating, healing, loving energy. Thank it for doing its best.

- You might imagine your Ideal Parent lovingly caring for this part of who you are. You are strong enough, confident enough, and powerful enough to love it all. It's all okay.

- Remember to breathe.

Do this meditation often until you notice your mindset towards yourself and your barriers softening. Pay attention to how loving and welcoming all of yourself affects your creativity, confidence, and energy.

Prompt ~ Unbidden Treasures ☑

Writing Exercise
Tools: Your *Leap Journal* and a pen
Time: 20 minutes

In addition to hiding from our own imperfections, sometimes we also hide from our own dreams and desires, especially when we are not sure if they are possible or if we have what it takes.

Even when we avoid our dreams and wishes, these still exist even if only in our unconscious awareness or memories. It can be helpful to consciously decide if we want to release them (and grieve them as necessary), pursue them, or wait to see how they may be changing or evolving.

Using your *Leap Journal*:

- Write a list of all the dreams you have ever had for your life. Include everything that comes to mind. Remember to include all your dreams from childhood.

- Next to each dream on your list write an L for let go, a D for do, and a W for wait.

- Ask yourself what will help you honor your choices through action. (The prompts on the following pages can help.)

Prompt ~ Alternate Lives ♥

Writing Exercise
Tools: Your *Leap Journal* and a pen
Time: 10 minutes

For this prompt, we are going to tap the power of our dreams by accessing our imagination.

Choose one of your dreams from your *Unbidden Treasures* list from the previous page that sounds like fun but seems unreachable.

- Write a fictional story, draw, paint a picture, or make a video of yourself being interviewed as if you have already achieved these dreams. Let yourself act as if you are as daring and successful as you always dreamed.

- What does that feel like? What would be fun about living that dream?

- What about this dream might help you achieve what you want for yourself and your life?

- What might be difficult? What about this dream might keep you from fully experiencing what you want for yourself and your life?

You can also do this prompt by simply closing your eyes.

- In a meditative state, imagine achieving the dream you chose. Let yourself fully experience what it would feel like to have achieved that specific dream.

Write down any insights you gain in your *Leap Journal.*

Prompt ~ Do One Thing ☑

Writing Exercise + Weekly Practice
Tools: Your *Leap Journal*, a pen, and any tools related to your "one thing"
Time: One week

This prompt is designed to support you in exploring a dream that still interests you, no how impractical it may seem for your own life.

Look back over your *Unbidden Treasures* list and circle any dreams that still interest you. Next, brainstorm some small steps you can take this week to rekindle whatever it was about that dream that appealed to you.

- Make a list in your *Leap Journal* of all the ideas you come up with, even if they seem silly or impractical.

For example, if your dream was becoming an actor, you might sign up for an acting class at your local community college, recite a poem for your best friend over zoom, or perform a monologue about an event in your life for loved ones. If you always wanted to paint, you could buy yourself a paint set, or box of children's finger paints.

- Choose one action step from your list to do this week. You might want to continue this over a period of time, doing one action step each week for a month or year.

Something magical and powerful happens when we honor and acknowledge our yearnings, even if in a simple way. We can awaken and trigger a creative energy that can be very powerful.

One thing leads to the next. While we might not see the road ahead, honoring our hidden desires through small actions can welcome in unexpected, positive opportunities.

Prompt ~ Have a Funeral ♥

Movement Exercise
Tools: A rock, magic markers or paint and paintbrush, nature
Time: One hour

Any loss we experience in life can take up emotional and energetic space, draining and distracting us from doing other things that bring us positive energy. We can grieve lost dreams just like we grieve loved ones who have left our lives.

If there are any dreams on your list that you really resonated with at some point in your life, it can be very powerful to honor these unmet dreams in some ceremonial act.

- Find a rock in nature and decorate it with words and images related to an unfulfilled dream. Perhaps include a message to this dream, as if it was a real being.

- Take this rock to some place in nature, such as to a lake, river, ocean, or private space like a park or your backyard.

- Thank this dream for coming into your life.

- Thank the version of you who at one time really wanted this dream to come true.

- Then, throw the rock into the body of water or bury it under the earth, setting it free.

- Another way to do this prompt is to display this rock somewhere special like on an altar or in your garden, to honor the part of yourself who once wanted this dream to come true.

Treat the act of letting this dream go as sacred, like how you would honor the loss of someone you love. Let the version of you who truly wanted this dream to come true to grieve. Letting go can free up space so the part of you who had this desire can dream a new dream that is in your highest good *now*.

Letting go makes space for the people we are evolving into and becoming. Every loss makes room for a new beginning. Pay attention to anything new that comes into your life after doing this prompt, whether an energy or mood shift, or a new opportunity or friend.

> "*Sometimes when you let go of a broken dream, another one gently takes its place.*"
>
> ~*Melody Beattie*

Pain

I didn't know
it was going to be this hard.

She plops down
something heavy,
sterile white background
behind her,
stainless steel
hospital bed.

She looks tired, drained.

I thought this thing
called life
would be much easier.

But it's not, is it?

It's hard at moments,
hard like glass
cutting into
preciousness.

Where softness
and laughter
should be
sometimes
drips

Pain.

Prompt ~ Singing Hard ☀

Writing + Musical Activity
Tools: A private place, your *Leap Journal*, a pen, and a musical instrument
Time: 30 minutes

Facing our blocks lessens their power and can help us find creative pathways through difficult experiences. Think of something in your life right now that feels "hard as glass." It might be your own thoughts or a firm stance you or someone else has taken on an issue. It could also be a person whose rigidity, judgements, or communication style makes it difficult for you to remember your own preciousness.

Hardness might appear in other ways too, for example in the form of a task that is overly challenging, or something that feels out of place, such as clutter that's blocking your flow, or an obligation keeping you from doing something you love. You might also notice hardness showing up as a metaphor, for example, like cracked concrete next to a field of flowers, or a building that doesn't fit in with the surrounding architecture.

Write a song to whatever is showing up as hard in your life in the form of a conversation. You might begin:

- *You are difficult, but I know the truth…*
- *If only you…*
- *I know you are trying hard to…*
- *Thank you for…*

You might sing your song at the top of your lungs, in the shower, or to a friend. Don't worry about how your song sounds. Let writing your song be *easy* (not hard) and fun!

> *"If someone comes along and shoots an arrow into your heart, it's fruitless to stand there and yell at the person. It would be much better to turn your attention to the fact that there's an arrow in your heart..."*
>
> *~Pema Chodron*

Hello, Critic

Look at you there,
Critic that you are.

What do you think,
really?

Come closer.
Go on.
Critique it.
I dare you.

Hate and love,
it's all the same.

I am not afraid.

Come closer so
I can see
the judgement in your eye.

You,
up close and personal,
reflect back
yourself.

You,
like a mirror
for my
Inner Challenger,
Critic
Judge.

How good do you feel now
as you gaze upon your own
self-made image?

So happy that you
have castrated me?

Wouldn't it have been easier
to create something too?

Creators, artists, poets,
please keep creating
something that has never been.

Who cares what they think?

Each mark,
each magic,
is as sacred as the
first heartbeat,
the first movement of life
within the seed.

You know this

And so do they.

That's why they gather
like moths to your flames.

They want to remember
they have this too.

So, keep creating.

Maybe someday,
their hearts will thaw
and they too will join
the great waterfall of joy
that is this thing called Art.

Until then,
for God's sake,
just keep creating.

Prompt ~ Hello Critic ♥

Art Project
Tools: Your *Leap Journal*, a pen, crayons, paints, or colored pencils.
Time: 30 minutes

This prompt is about bringing your Inner Critics, who usually work unconsciously, into conscious form. Our Inner Critics are simply versions of our ego-selves we keep modifying to protect ourselves as we live increasingly complicated lives.

Just as we use our creativity to respond to, adapt, and constantly modify our ego-selves, we can also use our creativity to heal and change these parts of ourselves to be more helpful. When we soften and use the power of play, we often discover that our Inner Critics are not monsters, but instead, can evolve and change just like the rest of us.

First, however, it's important to start with accepting how our Inner Critics are in this moment. Choose an Inner Critic who has been particularly troublesome for you. Using art supplies, creatively personify the energy of this Inner Critic and the role it plays in your life. You might want to paint a picture, draw a sketch, make a character out of clay, or write a paragraph describing it.

Honor your own inner truth. Describe how this part of yourself makes you feel and what you know it as. You might choose to personify your Inner Critic like the ogre or a monster in a children's story or horror movie. If you recognize anyone you know as you explore the identity of this Inner Critic, it's okay. We tend to internalize people or characters we meet in the outer world, whether in films or stories, or real people especially if they affected us emotionally.

When we soften and use the power of play, we often discover that our Inner Critics are not monsters, but instead simply energy, ready to become something new.

Have fun with this prompt. Let your imagination run wild. Remember, you cannot do this wrong.

- What does this Inner Critic look like?
- What do they sound like?
- What do they act like?
- What made them this way?
- What is their name?
- Once you've portrayed your Inner Critic, say "I see you."
- Do you have more than one version of an Inner Critic? (Most of us have several.) If so, feel free to repeat this prompt and create all the members of your Critique Team.
- What are some "new and improved" versions of these Inner Critics you might prefer instead? Use your imagination to design new jobs or personalities for them. How might they want to grow or change?

Prompt ~ How Dare You ♥

Writing Project
Tools: Your *Leap Journal* and a pen
Time: 20 minutes

It's impossible to control how people respond to what we put out into the world. We can, however, control the extent to which we allow it to impact our own sense of self by setting our own inner boundaries. Sometimes, however, before taking control of our inner perspective, we first need to provide an outlet for how we feel.

For this prompt, write a letter to your Inner Critic, or anyone who ever criticized or judged you in a way that has stayed with you. Begin your letter with:

- *How dare you…*
  Say everything on paper you wish you could have said to them in person.

After you've got all your complaints off your chest, write:

- *Instead, I wish you would have…*
  Offer them constructive ideas on how they could have spent their precious words and energy instead.

After writing this letter, do one positive thing to honor and celebrate yourself, your dreams, the part of your personality that they criticized harshly, or something you have created. You might frame a favorite photo of yourself, maybe of you as a child. Or you might display or share one of your creations. You might post a poem you wrote on social media, or share your creative dreams with a trusted friend. Or perhaps you will spend some time doing the activity your critics judged you for. We scare our inner ogres away by reclaiming our gifts, regardless of what our critics might say.

You have unique gifts to offer the world that no one else can. When we take creative leaps and actions that celebrate our gifts, we energetically send the message that nothing can stop us from sharing our light with the world.

No matter what anyone else thinks, you, your unique gifts, and your creativity are important and valuable. After doing this prompt, do something comforting for yourself. Get a cup of tea, take a nap, go for a peaceful nature walk, etc.

Prompt ~ Wounded Child ♥

Meditation
Tools: A private, quiet place
Time: 20 minutes

The most effective way to lessen the power of our inner and outer critics is through love, acceptance, and insight.

Option 1 ~ Hug Your Critic as Child

Imagine what your Inner Critic could have been like as a young child.

- Close your eyes and imagine taking this childlike version of your Inner Critic in your arms and giving him, her, or them a big hug.

Option 2 ~ Hug Your Younger Self

Imagine *yourself* as a child before any criticism ever entered your being. Imagine giving this younger version of *you* a hug.

- What message or words of wisdom might you offer your younger self?

- No matter what has come your way, you have made it through life's many challenges to where you are today. You are still the same beautiful person filled with light that you have always been, since the day you were born. You are resilient and miraculous, and you were then too.

Prompt ~ Soft Lullaby ☀

Writing + Musical Activity
Tools: Your *Leap Journal*, a pen, and a private, quiet place.
Time: 20 minutes

Imagine yourself when you were a baby or young toddler. Write a lullaby offering comfort, encouragement, and confidence to this younger version of you.

- What does it feel like to connect with this younger self?
- What are some gifts, information, protection, or wisdom that might have helped your younger self feel more peaceful or confident?
- Imagine this goodness and protection flowing out to your younger self as you sing or read the words you have written.

> "*Many blocked people are actually very powerful and creative personalities who have been made to feel guilty about their own strengths and gifts.*"
>
> *~Julia Cameron*

Crap

I think it's crap,
this writing.

Simple.
Clunky.
Uninspired.

Yet I've learned to
write it all down
and keep it.

Because sometimes
the phrases that
roll around on my tongue
like a pearl in an oyster,
the next day
become like sand,
gritty in my teeth.

And sometimes
clunky hard tools
once thought
rusty and wrong
for the task
I later learn
are actually

The Rarest of Gems.

Prompt ~ Rarest of Gems ♥

Writing Exercise
Tools: Your *Leap Journal* and a pen
Time: 20 minutes + one week

Have you ever created something that you thought was amazing, only to look at it the next day and see it from a very different, more negative, or judgmental view?

How about the opposite? Have you ever thought something you've created was awful, only to be told by someone else that they loved it, or to look at it with fresh eyes after time passed and decide it wasn't half bad?

So much of how we judge ourselves is subjective, based on the current time or space. This prompt can be particularly useful to do when you are preparing to make a big change in your life that involves others, or before releasing a creation to the public.

Choose something someone else has created like a favorite book or well-loved movie.

Write two reviews:

- Write one that is scathing and judgmental.

- Write a second one that is a raving positive review.

Read what you have written, then:

- Throw the negative review away, burn it, or safely get rid of it.

- Read the positive review out loud to yourself daily for one month, pretending it is about something *you* created. (Alter it as needed for this purpose.)

- Notice what happens. Record any insights in your *Leap Journal*.

Prompt ~ Three Perspectives ♥

Meditation + Writing Exercise
Tools: Your *Leap Journal* and a pen
Time: 30 minutes (about 10 minutes per story)

When we see the world or ourselves through only one lens, life can feel very small and stuck. When we soften and loosen our grip on how things are supposed to be, we start to open, and new doors and opportunities often do too. For this prompt, we are going to experiment with this idea of there being many different possibilities for our lives, including many ways of doing what we do.

Think of some area of your life that is problematic for you, or has been in the past. Perhaps the way you are doing something doesn't seem to be working right, or you are having trouble in a relationship or at your job. What you choose isn't as important as what happens internally when you do this exercise. You can choose to do this as a meditation exercise, with your eyes closed, as a writing exercise, or as both.

Explore what is happening, or what has happened from the viewpoint of the following three characters:

Character 1 ~ House Fly's View

Zoom in and see the situation from the perspective of an actual "fly on the wall" who can buzz about and see everything from close-up. Pay special attention to small details, such as how things look, what you hear, how each person seems to be feeling, or anything else the fly notices.

Character 2 ~ Eagle's View

Zoom out and see the situation from the perspective of an eagle flying above the scene who can see for many miles. Pay attention to the big picture, who is coming and going, and anything that is happening far away from the scene that might be important. Imagine that this eagle cannot only see for many miles, but also has a long-distance view of events that happened before and after the event as well.

Character 3 ~ Angel's View

Now see the situation from the perspective of an all-loving, all-knowing spiritual guide or angel who always sees the good within each person. This angel also can see the positive gifts, miracles, and spiritual significance of all that humans experience. Whether you believe in angels, spiritual guides, or God is not important for this prompt. Instead, simply imagine what an angel might have witnessed or known about the event.

If you ever find yourself feeling stuck, you might want to repeat this exercise and see how it shifts your perspective, or what new insights you gain.

Prompt ~ Foe, Friend, and Acquaintance ♥

Writing Exercise
Tools: Your *Leap Journal* and a pen
Time: 20 minutes

This prompt is like the previous one but has to do with individuals rather than a past event. Think of a person who is problematic for you, either now or who was in the past.

For this prompt, you are being invited to write three paragraphs describing this person, each from a very different perspective.

Option 1 ~ Foe

Write from the perspective of someone who hates this person or sees them as a threat.

- Begin with: *(Insert name)* is bad news. I knew it from the first minute…

Option 2 ~ Friend

Write from the perspective of someone who adores this person, like their best friend, lover, or parent.

- Begin with: *(Insert name)* has always been special. I love how…

Option 3 ~ Acquaintance

Write from the perspective of someone who has just met this person for the first time and is very curious about them.

- Begin with: *(Insert name)* is a mystery. I'm so curious about...

As you write, notice how you feel. Record any insights in your *Leap Journal.*

> *"The voyage of discovery is not in seeking new landscapes, but in having new eyes."*
>
> *~Marcel Proust*

Uncomfortable

I've stopped telling the truth
because I can tell it makes them feel
uncomfortable.

I ask myself:

Why?

Why do I need to share all that?

Insecurity?

Desire overrun?

Or a yearning
to be known
and know
and say,
let's get beyond
all of this
idle chit chat and be
real?

Either way,
I think I'll hit pause.

They don't seem ready for it.

Yet.

Prompt ~ Who's Ready for You? ♥

Writing Exercise
Tools: Your *Leap Journal* and a pen
Time: 20 minutes

Sometimes those who have judged us most harshly in our lives or who continue to do so are just not ready for what we want to share. Witnessing our journey or gifts may trigger something in them, such as unhealed pain that they would rather not feel, and may not even be aware of or able to name.

On the other hand, we are all on different paths and have different needs, wants, and perspectives. Not everyone is going to want what we have to offer for a myriad of reasons that have nothing to do with us. When we share ourselves or our creations with the wrong audience, we can feel disappointed, or the flow of our lives can become unnecessarily blocked.

- Make a list of your safe people when it comes to sharing the most tender aspects of your personality or life story, or creations that are most sacred or important to you.

- Make a second list of your unsafe people, or people who may not yet be able to clearly understand your true intentions or the value of what you have to offer.

Keep in mind that just because someone doesn't fully understand what you have created doesn't mean their perspective is a true reflection of how others will see it, or its worth. Your list of safe and unsafe people may also change over time the more you come to understand, love, and accept yourself.

Wisdom is having the ability to know which aspects of ourselves to share with whom, and to stop looking in the wrong places for what we need. Wisdom is also knowing and honoring when *we* are ready to share our creations with specific people or audiences, regardless of whether they are to receive them.

> *"What we're talking about is getting to know fear, becoming familiar with fear, looking it right in the eye – not as a way to solve problems, but as a complete undoing of old ways of seeing, hearing, smelling, tasting, and thinking."*
>
> *~Pema Chodron*

Blocked

The minute we say

"It's worthless!"

Pop!

Like an air balloon
above our heads,

the poem disappears

as if it never was.

Prompt ~ Unblocked ♥

Writing Exercise
Tools: Your *Leap Journal* and a pen
Time: 20 minutes

Think of a project or dream you abandoned at some point because you didn't think your creations or you were good enough, or you didn't think you had what it took to succeed.

Write down the name of this dream in your *Leap Journal*.

- Pretend the part of yourself who wanted to do this project is a fictional character. How old are they? What are their passions? What might their personality be like? Do they have a name?

- What is something simple and creative you can do to honor this version of you that had that idea or dream? Perhaps buy yourself a gift, do a creative project like the idea you had in the past, or do something to explore the idea, for example, by perusing your local library or the Internet.

- Is there any aspect of that dream, idea, or project you want to spend your time on again, just for fun?

- Make a plan. Schedule it in your calendar. Write it down.

"The only thing we are ever dealing with is a thought, and a thought can be changed."

~Louise Hay

Crazy

Crazy?
I've been called worse.

Boring?
Yes, well, one needs to be.
Sitting still is how the magic comes.

Backwards?
Sometimes I even forget
my own name
and that
stirring a pot
is how food
is made.

Weak?
Only before strong currents
that want to take me
to new places.

To them I say:

Let me set sail
and carry me!

Prompt ~ Going Places ☀

Art Project
Tools: Your *Leap Journal*, a pen, crayons, magic markers, or colored pencils
Time: 30 minutes

What are some of the new directions you would like to take your life, your work, your dreams, your relationships, or your creative hobbies?

- Draw a map of a fictitious new world. Label all the imaginary land masses with names of projects, directions, or themes you've dreamed of exploring creatively.

- You might include names of songs or books you'd love to write, hobbies you'd like to try, or topics you don't know much about but that interest you.

- Now draw a fictitious figure, a simple stick figure or cartoon character who is going to visit all these creative places. How will they travel—by foot, by boat, by different vehicles depending on the terrain? Where will they go first? What will they need for their journey?

You could also write a story, song, or poem about the adventures this creative traveler will have. If this exercise feels silly or even crazy, that's good. Creative leaps often do!

> *"The stream is saved from the sluggishness of its current by the perpetual opposition of the soil through which it must cut its way."*
>
> *~Rabindranath Tagore*

Hiding

Tucked in tight
so no one
would notice

At least,
not enough
to care

Now I know
the only one
I was really
hiding from
was
Myself.

Cloaked and tucked

Buried so deep that
I could not hear

My own true voice.

Prompt ~ Gone Hiding ♥

Writing Exercise + Art Project
Tools: Your *Leap Journal* and a pen
Time: 20 minutes

Remember how much fun it was to hide when you were young? What would it be like to be able to retreat or become invisible whenever you wanted?

This idea of hiding out or becoming invisible can be very powerful. It can be very healing to know that there is a safe place we can go to get away from the rest of the world for a bit, to take a break.

- What would your ideal hiding spot or retreat place be right now at this point in your life?
- Where would it be?
- What would you stock it with?
- Would there be a bed or place to rest? A desk or workplace?
- How would you get there?
- When would you use it? How often could you imagine using it to rest, recharge, and retreat? Let your imagination run wild as you invent this special place, designed just for you.

Describe and sketch your ideal hiding place in your *Leap Journal*.

Prompt ~ Out of Hiding ♥

Writing Exercise + Meditation
Tools: Your *Leap Journal* and a pen
Time: 30 minutes

We all have ways we protect ourselves from the outer world, strategies we use to take a break. Answer the following questions in your *Leap Journal*:

- What is an area of your life where you've been hiding?
- What is a strategy you use when you need privacy or want to be anonymous?
- Is there another strategy that might be more effective or helpful?
- What would happen if you came out of hiding?
- What might change in your life if you were willing to be seen more fully by others?
- What are benefits of coming out of hiding? What is a gift that hiding offers you?
- What are possible risks? What can't happen if you stay in hiding?
- What is one way you could safely experiment with being more fully seen?

- What is your best-case scenario story about letting yourself be seen in a new way? Describe it as fully as possible. What would you love to have happen?

Meditation

- Close your eyes and imagine what it would feel like if your best-case scenario about coming out of hiding or being fully seen were to come true.

> *"You may be moved in a direction you do not understand, away from the safe, the familiar, toward a vision that is blurry, yet still pounds against the doors of your dreams."*
>
> *~Susan Rogers Norton*

Child's Mind

Something is
about to happen.

I can feel it.

I don't know how I know,
But I do.

I feel it in the air.
A change.
A big transition.

I don't know if I like it.

Or is it just that I've had too much caffeine?

Jitters.
I'm shaking.

It rolls
across the plain like an
earthquake's coming.

If I know bad news
before it happens.

Is it all my fault?

Prompt ~ Not Your Fault ☑

Writing Exercise
Tools: Your *Leap Journal*, a pen, and a friend
Time: 30 minutes

When we were children, we often thought we were the cause of things that were not our fault. This was developmentally natural; we were still learning where our boundaries ended and those of others began. Our well-being was inextricably linked to the well-being of our caregivers.

Sometimes as adults, we continue patterns from childhood that are no longer in our best interest. Enmeshment or confusion about boundaries and what is our responsibility can run deep.

Answer the following questions in your *Leap Journal*:

- What is something in your life that is taking a lot of your energy?
- Is this really your problem to solve?
- Who else might be responsible or might be able to help?
- Are you trying to protect anyone? Whom? Why?
- To what extent is this person capable of taking care of themselves?
- What would happen if you changed your approach to this challenge?
- How would your time and energy levels change?

- What emotional needs do you have that are not being met?
- What are some direct requests you could make of others that might help?
- What are some new ways you can take care of yourself?
- What are some changes you would like to make in how you care for, protect, or relate to others?
- What are some changes you are ready to make regarding how you take care of your own needs?
- Are there any events that happened in the past that you took responsibility for, which were not your fault?
- What can you do differently today to let go of this responsibility or burden?

Write it down. Share your insights with a trusted friend, therapist, healer, coach, or loved one.

> *"I used to spend so much time reacting and responding to everyone else that my life had no direction…Once I realized it was okay for me to think about and identify what I wanted, remarkable things began to take place in my life."*
>
> *~Melody Beattie*

What A Bitch

I've started to not take things
quite so personally.

I don't know how it happened, really,
since that's a fault of mine–
thinking everything's about me.

I think it has something to do with
having teenagers.

When they push away,
roll their eyes and
challenge what I say,
I've learned
all they really want
is to know
that they will be okay
on their own someday.

They are practicing.

And they need to,
to find their way.

I only know this because I was one once.

Or maybe it's because now,
I pick my head up more often
and see Unhappy
before it gets here.

So I know
misery happens
for reasons
that don't have to do with me.

The real reason may be
because now that I am writing,
I remember what a bitch I could be
when I wasn't.

Prompt ~ Let Life Flow ☑

Writing Exercise
Tools: Your *Leap Journal*, a pen, and tools for your chosen hobby
Time: One week

Research shows that hobbies and experiencing a flow state—that zone we enter when we are so engaged in doing something we love that we lose track of time—can be incredibly healing. For this prompt, set aside a week where you spend a few minutes each day doing something related to a creative hobby. Being in flow can be like a door, opening the way for a greater sense of purpose and passion in our lives.

You might revisit a hobby you loved as a child or try an activity you've always been curious about but for which you thought you didn't have enough time, was too complicated, or perhaps too silly. Your activity could be as simple as doodling or coloring in an adult coloring book.

At the start of the week, make some notes about how things are going in your life:

- What's working and what's not, especially when it comes to your happiness, perspective, and sense of confidence?

After the week, do another self-assessment:

- What if anything has changed?
- How is nurturing your creativity good for you?
- What is the easiest, simplest way to bring flow into your life on a regular basis?

> *"Art is my cure to all this madness, sadness and loss of belonging in the world and through it I'll walk myself home."*
>
> *~Nikki Rowe*

Piranhas

There are piranhas out there
hovering, waiting to inhale
and ingest
anything we put out.

Poor, starved beings
roaming for scraps
if only they looked
inside.

Now we have a choice.

We can lean out,
looking for trouble,
or we can lean inward instead.

Knowing that
no one can ever
take from us
the wellspring of Creativity
that overflows
and is who we are.

No one can take your Soul
and make it their own,
try as they might.

So, rest.

Forget all that.

Watch your back.

Turn away from piranhas.

But mostly, keep your ear
tuned to the ground
listening for the vibration
of footsteps coming

Your next great
Inspiration
with no other name
than
your Self.

Prompt ~ When They Get Mad ♥

Writing Exercise
Tools: Your *Leap Journal* and a pen
Time: 10 minutes

A friend of mine had a great parenting one-liner. When her kids complained about mistreatment by a friend or bully, she would reply: "Sounds like they took out their mad on you!"

Most of us give our critics far more power than they deserve. In most cases, people who hurt us were simply experiencing their own bad moods and we unknowingly showed up at the wrong time.

We all experience anger and when we do, we rarely do, say things, or act in ways that we would if we were not triggered. How we react is never about *who* we are, but rather, reflects how we are feeling. It can be difficult to remember this in the moment, however.

For this prompt, think of someone who has hurt you in the past, or towards whom you still have a grudge or hurt feelings.

Complete the following sentences in your *Leap Journal*:

- When they are mad, they…
- When I am mad, I…

After you have finished, reread what you have written. Following each completed sentence, add the words:

"…and I'm still okay."

Prompt ~ You Are Safe ♥

Meditation
Tools: Your *Leap Journal* and a pen
Time: 20 minutes

Personal conflicts often take huge amounts of energy that can distract us from hearing our own intuition and taking positive leaps forward. When we have encounters with difficult people in our lives, we often do something that I call the ***Blame-Shame-Name Game.*** Here's how it works:

- **Blame:** We might *blame* the other person for what happened, building them up as our enemy

- **Shame:** We might *shame* ourselves, using the event as evidence of why we are unworthy, do not deserve joy, or are unworthy of taking leaps.

- **Name:** we might boost up our own *name* to make ourselves feel superior to others, to avoid feelings of insecurity, vulnerability, or fear.

Without tools, support, or a commitment to heal the underlying pain that led to the conflict and our resulting emotional reactions, we may feel as if we are constantly at war, even if the conflict happened long ago or the other person is no longer a threat.

Think of someone whom you see as a threat to your own emotional or physical well-being, or who once hurt you in some way. Following is a meditation designed to soften and heal the underlying pain associated with difficult people or events in our lives. Depending on your unique situation, you may want to get professional support with this process.

Do this meditation as often as you need to, keeping the focus on yourself and your intention to accept yourself and your own feelings with caring and compassion, rather than the details of the story. When we accept anything just as it is, including our own pain, it usually shifts, heals, evolves, and transforms into something new.

- Close your eyes.

- Notice how you are feeling.

- When you think of this person or past event, what do you feel in your body?

- Take a deep breath. Breathe in. Breathe out.

- Label any sensations. See if you can describe each feeling with a color, image, or word.

- If thoughts come up about what you are feeling, you might label your stories with a one-word summary like rejected, sad, hope, attraction, excitement, etc., then return to focusing on your breath.

- Imagine sending love, compassion, and a deep sense of caring to your emotions, almost as if they are young children.

- See if any creative ideas come to you about how you can soften the energy around any feelings in your body, making more space and allowing them to be exactly as they are.

- Remember to breathe. Breathe in. Breathe out.

- End this meditation whenever you feel a positive shift, or a sense of peace or softness.

Remember, we all have uncomfortable feelings. They are not a sign of being bad or good, just confirmation that we are human, just like everyone else.

Loving awareness can lead to dramatic changes in our lives, inner peace, and well-being. Sometimes these happen gradually over time, without us even realizing they are happening. Other times, changes can happen suddenly, interrupting a mood or habitual pattern and feeling like a miracle.

This meditation can be helpful while experiencing positive emotions as well as challenging ones.

Prompt ~ Accepting Your Emotions 

Writing Exercise
Tools: Your *Leap Journal* and a pen
Time: 20 minutes

Processing painful past events can take valuable energy that we could use instead to generate new, more positive experiences. Before we can really let go, however, we often need to grieve that we didn't receive what we may have expected, wanted, or needed in the past. Grieving is basically a deep form of acceptance. Grieving shifts our inner dialogue from one of blame, judgement, or investigation to taking care of the only thing that is our responsibility—healing our emotions. While it's not always pleasant, grieving is often far more effective than trying to change what isn't ours to change, or seeking answers that are not ours to know.

Think of a difficult interaction or event that didn't go the way you wish it had. Complete the following sentences in your *Leap Journal:*

- An experience that was very difficult for me was...
- When I think of the other person/people involved I feel...
- I wish this had happened differently...
- I am sad that...
- Deep down inside, I really wanted...

After doing this prompt, comfort yourself in some caring way. Take a walk, read a good book, get a warm cup of tea, or take a nap. Do something nurturing for yourself the way your Ideal Parent would.

Prompt ~ Welcoming Unwelcome Gifts 

Writing Exercise
Tools: Your *Leap Journal*, a pen, and a friend
Time: 20 minutes

When difficult situations happen, they almost always offer us gifts, even if we would not have chosen the form in which the gift arrived if we had been given the choice.

The more we allow ourselves to feel emotions linked to unwelcome events in our lives, the more we unlock the gifts these experiences offered us. While we don't have control over the behavior of others, the wisdom we gain from witnessing others' choices is always ours; nothing anyone can ever do can ever take away the internal wisdom or gifts we gained from outer events.

Examples of such gifts might include the ability to set better boundaries, a better understanding of how people act when they are triggered, gratitude for our good times or blessings, new creative ideas and insights, or learned empathy.

For this prompt, think of a conflict or negative interaction you had with someone in your life. Complete the following sentences in your *Leap Journal:*

- As a result of this event, I now know…
- I learned this about myself…
- I learned this about people in general…
- I learned this about life in general…

- As a result of this experience, I now do this differently…
- Something positive that probably never would have happened if this event hadn't occurred is…
- Since this event, I have been…
- I am grateful that…
- I am wiser since this event happened because…
- This event taught me that I am strong in these ways…
- This event helped me realize that one of my gifts is…
- Something I know for sure about this event is…
- Something I'm still integrating from this event is…

Claiming and integrating wisdom gained from painful experiences can help us to let go of resentments that may be blocking our creative flow. Emotional healing can take time and happen differently for each of us depending on our unique stories and situations. If you feel big emotions when experimenting with this prompt, you may want to get support from a trusted friend, trained healer, or therapist.

It can be helpful to tell a trusted person about any new insights you gain from doing this prompt. Having our wisdom witnessed is yet another way we can claim the gifts we have gained.

Having a Do-Over ♥

Meditation
Tools: You
Time: 20 minutes

Sometimes when I find myself talking to my kids in tone that I know is not helpful, I'll say something like, "Let's reset. I'd like to try again. Let's have a *do-over*." I might even playfully walk out of the room then back in again.

While we don't always have the luxury to do this or might only realize that things were going down a bad path in hindsight, the good news is, we can always have a *do-over* in our imaginations. This is true even if a difficult interpersonal encounter occurred decades before.

For this meditation, we are going to go back in time and have a fictious *do-over*. Some believe imagining more positive outcomes to past events reprograms the way our bodies log those memories, potentially changing future outcomes.

For this meditation, think of an interpersonal event that you wish had gone differently. Come up with your *do-over* plan before starting. That way you can avoid getting carried away by your emotions especially if the previous event triggers you.

Because this is *your* meditation, make sure your imaginary do-over plan focuses on what is in your best interest as far as an outcome. It is often surprising how lovingly making choices that are in our best interest, even in our imaginations, can positively affect our future relationships with others.

It can also help to remember that we are almost always making choices based on positive intentions, which are often the desire to be accepted, loved, or to connect, even if we sometimes try to have these met in ways that aren't graceful or skillful.

(If you find creative visualization difficult, you can also do this exercise as a creative writing prompt, describing everything you wish had happened in the present tense, like a fictional story that begins "I...")

- Close your eyes and deeply relax.

- Imagine being in a safe place where you are completely protected.

- Invite your True Self, a loving guide, Spirit, or an Ideal Parent to come and be with you during this meditation.

- When it feels right, imagine the person you have chosen to do a *do-over* with joins you in this safe space.

- In your imagination, ask this person if they are willing to have a do-over. If the answer is no, ask them if they are open to at least hearing what you wish had happened. (Remember, this is your meditation, your imagination. You are in charge of your inner experience.)

- If, even in your imagination, the other person doesn't seem open to hearing or experiencing your wishes for a do-over, that's okay. Ask them to leave, then instead imagine telling a fictitious Ideal Parent what you wish had happened instead. The most important thing is that you take care of your own needs in whatever way you can.

- If, in your imagination, the other person seems open to having a *do-over* then let the games begin! Imagine the past event going exactly the way you wish it had. Imagine receiving everything *you* wanted or needed, feeling respected, appreciated, and safe. Imagine setting the boundaries you wish you had and being heard. The more you can tap your creativity and convince your critical, rational mind that your ideal version of events is happening, the better.

- Wish the other person well.

- Before the end of the meditation, thank the other person for joining you, then ask them to leave the sacred space of your imagination.

- Imagine your True Self, guide, Spirit, or Ideal Parent giving you a hug, or anything else you may need.

- Imagine a healing white light cleansing you, almost as if you are taking a shower in a magical energy that can change negativity to positivity.

- Whenever it feels right, slowly and lovingly end your meditation.

Write down any insights you have in your *Leap Journal*.

Prompt ~ Reflecting the Enemy ☑

Writing Exercise
Tools: Your *Leap Journal* and a pen
Time: 20 minutes

The worst part of feeling stuck in a state of conflict is that it closes us off from the inner wisdom coming from other parts of ourselves. The truth is, we have a little bit of everyone and everything in us. This wholeness is part of being human. Integrating and accepting our diverse aspects of self is the key to inner peace.

Think of a relationship challenge you are currently having in your life.

- In your imagination, ask the person with whom you have had a conflict what advice they may have for you.

Remember, we're just dealing with our imagination not the real person; any wisdom you receive is coming from *you*, a part of your own creative mind that you rarely access.

- What advice do you agree with? (You might want to ask yourself, which part of you agrees?)

- What don't you agree with? (Again, consider which part of you disagrees, almost as if it is a fictious character.)

- How, if at all, might this advice help with a challenge you are currently having in your life?

Write down whatever comes to you in your *Leap Journal*.

> *"The people we are in relationship with are always a mirror, reflecting our own beliefs and simultaneously we are mirrors, reflecting their beliefs. So, relationship is one of the most powerful tools for growth."*
>
> *~Shakti Gawain*

Why Are You Surprised?

When she arrives,
small-minded
insecure,
judgmental,
grasping with
white knuckles
tightly to all she has left

I gasp
then turn away.

Yet why am I surprised?

Wouldn't it be
more healing
to simply nod
with a knowing smile
when she appears?

There she is.
There she is again.
I know her.

We are as much
the Tormented Soul
seeking that which
we forget
we already have
as we are

The God Within.

Prompt ~ You Are Miraculous ♥

Writing Exercise + Meditation
Tools: Your *Leap Journal* and a pen
Time: 10 minutes + one week

- Write a list in your *Leap Journal* of all the habits and traits you wish you didn't have.

- When you are done, imagine someone who loves you deeply and unconditionally, like an Ideal Parent, takes one look at your list of unwanted qualities, smiles, looks you in the eye, and explains how these are actually gifts in disguise, just some of the many reasons are why you are so very special and endearing to them.

- Now write a second list in your *Leap Journal* of your positive, good traits, those things you like about yourself. If you find this difficult to do, imagine what someone who loves you completely, like an Ideal Parent, partner, or best friend, might put on such a list.

- Read this "good" list before you go to bed every night for a week.

> "*Strengthen me by sympathizing with my strength, not my weakness.*"
>
> *~Amos Bronson Alcott*

I Don't Want To!

Feet planted
Straight back

Fists tight
at the ready

Oh, how I know that stance,
that battle cry!

Resisting what is good for us,
we all must have been
born ready
for this fight.

Will this rebel
stay to serve
when I finally remember
who I am?

And after so much practice,
fight with every bit of passion
to protect
my Soul?

Prompt ~ Setting Boundaries ☑

Writing Exercise + Meditation
Tools: Your *Leap Journal* and a pen
Time: Five minutes

When children say no, they often are very clear. The younger they are, the less apologetic and more honest they usually are when it comes to turning away from people who make them feel unsafe, or whom they simply don't like.

- Make a list of all the people who drain your energy, or who you know are not healthy for you to be around. This is your Boundaries List.

- Make a list of all those people who make you feel uplifted, happy, healthy, energetic, or valued just for being you. This is your YES List.

Write your answers to the following questions in your *Leap Journal:*

- How can you create stronger boundaries when it comes to the names on your Boundaries List?

- How can you make more time for the people on your YES List?

Repeat this exercise for places, foods, substances, drinks, environments, and activities.

The clearer we are about what is and isn't good for us and the more we respect this wisdom, the easier our lives flow.

Prompt ~ Loving Your Inner Child ♥

Writing Exercise + Meditation
Tools: Your *Leap Journal* and a pen
Time: 20 minutes

Sometimes, we are our own worst enemy. We might feel this way when we have trouble protecting ourselves from items or names on our Boundary Lists, or when we procrastinate tasks that are in our best interest.

Remember the movie *Big* where Tom Hanks played a young boy who made a wish to become a grown-up? After his dream came true, we witnessed an adult man going through life with a child's mind, emotions, and perceptions.

For this prompt, imagine that like Tom Hanks, you have an Inner Child in charge of the choices and decisions you make. Imagine hosting a conversation between your Ideal Parent and this Inner Child about tasks you may procrastinate or a habit you have been having trouble changing.

Your Inner Child Speaks

Using your non-dominant hand (for example if you are right-handed, use your left hand and if you are left-handed, use your right), complete the following sentences:

- I don't want to…
- I also don't want to…
- I don't understand why you're making me do…

- What I really want to do instead is…
- More than anything I need…
- I also wish…
- If I were really in charge I would…
- I think the best answer is…

Your Ideal Parent Speaks

Read what you have written, as if you are this child's perfect, Ideal, all-loving Parent. Imagine your Ideal, perfectly loving Parent takes your Inner Child's hand and thanks them for sharing.

Using your dominant hand, (right if you are right-handed, left if you are left-handed), complete the following sentences:

- I didn't realize that…
- I am glad I now know…
- I'm especially glad you told me…
- I like your idea about…
- I love your…
- I need…
- I want…

- I think...
- I want you to know...
- I promise to...

Write your insights in your *Leap Journal*.

Meditation

This prompt also can be very powerful as a meditation. Visualize your Ideal Parent and Inner Child meeting and connecting in a loving way. At the end of this creative visualization, you might imagine your Ideal Loving Parent giving your inner child a hug and the inner child accepting all the parent's love.

This visualization/creative writing exercise can be a very powerful way to integrate many different aspects of yourself, and to make positive changes from a state of acceptance and wholeness.

> *"Listen close to me... Anything can happen, child. Anything can be."*
>
> *~Shel Silverstein*

Two Voices

I have two voices
in my mind.

One says,
"There, there,
everything's fine."

"Everything works out just as it should."

The other tells a much more
dastardly tale about
villains and things going awry.

Some days I trust one.
Some, the other.

Which one hits the page

Today

Will tell my story
and write my life.

Prompt ~ Meet Your Inner Worrier 

Writing Exercise + Art Project
Tools: Your *Leap Journal*, a pen, and colored pencils
Time: 20 minutes

We all have those moments when we start thinking about worst-case scenarios instead of positive options for our lives. We often do this as a survival instinct, to keep ourselves and our loved ones safe. Sometimes, our internal dialogue goes on overdrive, and we start ruminating or thinking repetitive thoughts that keep us from enjoying the present-day moment.

When we can create distance from our inner parts, they often start to soften and have less influence on our overall identity. Using the power of imagination, we can then start to connect in a deeper way to who we really are, moving through the world as our True Self or Ideal Parent instead.

Create a character in your mind who personifies the type of person (or character) who might be anxious, worry, or assume the worst. Examples of characters like this are Eeyore, the donkey in the *Winnie-the-Pooh* stories, and the Fear Character in the Pixar movie *Inside Out*. Have fun with developing your own "worry" character.

- Write a paragraph describing your Inner Worrier in your *Leap Journal*. You might also want to draw or sketch them. Make your depiction as detailed and real as you can. Include everything from what they wear, how they act, what they look like, where they live, etc. Give them a playful name like Anxious Anne or Nervous Ned.

You can go even deeper by describing what traumatic events may have happened to them to make them feel so worried. Have fun with this.

The next time you find yourself worrying or feeling anxious about something, pretend it's not you who is doing the worrying, but rather this sad anxious character or inner part of you whispering about all its worries and fears. See what happens and if this changes your inner dialogue.

Track any shifts in your *Leap Journal*.

Prompt ~ Healing Worries Meditation 

Meditation
Tools: A quiet, private place
Time: 10 minutes

The following creative visualization can help ease worries by tapping the power of a loving inner voice.

- Close your eyes.
- Take a few nice deep breaths.
- Imagine going to a safe space where you are completely protected.
- Invite this Inner Worrier to join you there.
- Tell them this is a safe space where they can deeply relax.
- Now imagine your Inner Worrier's Ideal Parent, who loves them completely and accepts them just as they are, joins them in this safe place.
- Invite your Ideal Parent to do or say anything that might comfort your Inner Worrier, or help them relax and feel safe.

"Embrace each challenge in your life as an opportunity for self-transformation."

~Bernie Siegel

Self-Reflection

~Flowing With Your Blocks~

Blocks can come in many forms. The most common is our tendency to prioritize outer distractions over what is in our own best interest. Blocks can also occur in the form of unconscious habits and patterns. We all have habitual ways of interacting with the world that can prevent us from hearing our true voice.

Sometimes patterns develop because of how we were raised, or strategies we created to address past challenges. We may unconsciously hold onto these patterns, thinking they can protect us in the future, without realizing they may instead be holding us back.

We can also feel stuck because of buried or hidden emotions. Sometimes these emotions are linked to traumas or difficult experiences that happened to us, our predecessors, parents, or ancestors that impacted our perceptions of who we are and what is possible for us. Even just the general societal message that we are not enough can block our creative flow.

It's important to remember that we can alchemize past pain into a superpower (such as wisdom or empathy) that no one can ever take away from us.

- What is something you've been told about your strengths?
- What are some new ways you can nurture your unique gifts?
- If your creative strengths or gifts were young children entrusted in your care, how could you help these children feel safe?

- What are some new strategies you could use to protect your creativity and intuition?
- What is one action step you can take towards nurturing your creative dreams?
- What are some new insights you've gained about how to move through your creative and intuitive blocks and let your life flow?

What's Your Leap?

What's one new way you can make space for your True Self?

Life

What gives your life meaning?

My father and I once got into a tense discussion about how to do dishes. "There are hundreds of ways to do any task," I piped up, feeling criticized for my inadequacy in not getting that night's meal scrubbed off the insides of a pot quite right.

He scoffed, partly, I like to believe, to get my goat, for there was a time when jockeying like this, playfully challenging each other's world views was the closest we got to each other.

At that moment in time, shortly after I had moved out on my own, I was young and eager to prove myself and my worth. He was methodically, mindfully finding comfort in the regularity and rhythm of the simple task of scrubbing a pot in their newly reclaimed kitchen.

I was standing at his sink, my hands immersed in soapy water, and he was hovering nearby. I'm pretty sure he truly didn't agree my methods were equal to his, especially not that night, in his home, his sink, his suds of soap. I had elbowed my way over trying to lift his burden and be a help, a nicety, I thought. I now realize, many decades later, that I was inserting myself where I hadn't been invited to go.

Now that he's been gone for more than a decade, and I've grown up a bit, I look at this experience very differently than I did at the time. I no longer give any thought to who was right or wrong, about my need to be heard or wanting to help. Instead, I focus on the details, all those little things I can't get back again, no matter how much I may want to.

It is the little things that I miss the most, the way his fingers looked as they grasped the sponge, the way his back straightened when he didn't agree, the way he hunched slightly when he'd had a hard day, bowing under the weight of bearing others' sadness, and the way he still found just enough energy to look up from whatever he was doing, his eyes sparkling as he joked and teased, victory after I had just taken his bait.

The more years I spend in the living, the more I realize how much of life truly is about all of this—our gestures, moments, rote routines like making food, putting out the dog, folding laundry, and scrubbing pots. It is the tasks that we all must do that define us, that are our true creations, the way in which we express our individuality as we go about our days, choosing with care the proper clothes, facial expressions, and to-dos to keep our lives humming along.

It is in the day-to-day living that we get to express and reveal how we are feeling, what we value, what we are thinking, and who we are in each moment to anyone who cares enough to notice. We may see our daily chores or other everyday-isms as obstacles, hurdles keeping us from pen and paper, canvas and paint, joy and play—I know I so often do. And yet, how often we forget that our lives are creativity in motion, each task an art that is only and fully ours, colorful filaments of inspiration we are weaving into something new.

Each task bears our signature because we have done it and it is who we are. Each choice we make when we are not writing, making, building, or playing becomes fodder for the next sentence or creation we will craft when we are.

"No trumpets sound when the important decisions of our life are made. Destiny is made known silently."

~Agnes de Mille

Build a Day

Building a day,
brick by brick,
like a tower

What will this day bring?

Is the foundation made of
soft mud
soon to cave in on itself
or solid ground
of gratitude,
restfulness,
insights,
and
inspiration?

Where will we take this
one space
between
sun up
and
sun down
that we've been given?

How do we
build a day?

Prompt ~ Your Best Day ☑

Writing Exercise
Tools: Your *Leap Journal* and a pen
Time: 10 minutes

We often live our lives on automatic pilot. Creating a plan is the first step towards following our intuition and living our best life.

Make two columns on a piece of paper.

- On the left, list everything you wish you could experience in each day.

- On the right, list all the strategies that could help you feel that way.

Be creative. Write down everything that comes to you.

- What's one simple thing you can do today to make your day better?

> *"Start where you are. Use what you have. Do what you can."*
>
> *~Arthur Ashe*

Red-Shouldered Hawk

Red shouldered hawk
flies down
with its talons
grazing
still waters
rustling tall grasses
sweeping to find
something to eat.

If only he knew
that I hang
on his every move
with a prayer,
taking his visit
as from the Big One
beyond.

I know his
mere presence
as a sign
that we are being watched.

Life is happening and
it is going to be
a good day.

Prompt ~Nature Signs ☀

Life Practice
Tools: A safe place to walk in nature and time alone
Time: 20 minutes + one week

Our intuitive mind often speaks to us in symbols. Sometimes this guidance comes to us internally, like in a dream or during a meditation. Other times, something in the outer world can remind us of something, or awaken our inner knowing. For example, we might associate something we see with a commonly-used metaphor, such as "sneaky as a fox" or a "storm brewing."

We also each have our own internal dictionary of symbols based on our personal memories and experiences.

- Take a walk in your neighborhood. If you were the character in a story, what could the signs and symbols you notice on your walk mean?

- Keep a daily journal tracking symbols you encounter.

- For one week, keep a notepad by your bedside and write down your dreams each morning. Make a special note of signs, symbols, images, and repeating themes.

- Trust your intuition about the meaning of the signs and symbols you notice.

> *"I do not at all understand the mystery of grace – only that it meets us where we are but does not leave us where it found us."*
>
> ~Anne Lamott

Time's Passing

In every hour
there is a moment
when the minute hand
clicks into place,
marking time
now
and we rest
in false
collusion
with the idea
that we know
where we are.

Life moves forward,
second by second,
millisecond by millisecond,
never in one place.

Nothing ever stops,
Really.

We know this
and yet,
how comforting a clock is
without a second hand
to mark
the passing of time.

Prompt ~ One Moment at a Time ☀

Mindfulness Activity
Tools: A quiet, private space, and a timer
Time: One minute

It used to take me one minute to warm our son's nightly cup of milk when he was young. I often would do quick tasks in the kitchen while I waited. I was amazed by how much I could get done in that short amount of time!

- Set a timer for one minute.
- Take a couple nice deep breaths.
- If you find your mind wandering, bring yourself back to your breath.
- Imagine light and love pouring down from above, flowing through the crown of your head into every inch of your body, and being released through the bottom of your feet.

After the minute is up, how do you feel?

> *"If we take care of the moments, the years will take care of themselves."*
>
> *~Maria Edgeworth*

In Two Places

I cannot be in two places at one time.

And yet, "Am I?"
she asks,
folding laundry,
checking lists
dog whining
all the while aware
of clouds moving overhead.

"I cannot be two places
at one time,"
she whispers to her child
who asks for something,
that one more thing
tipping madness into
a simple day.

"I cannot be two places at one time,"
she says,
trying to keep
mindful simplicity,
one foot in front of the other,
one step at a time.

We all know
this is what keeps us sane.

Yet, I lie.

I'm always in more places
at one time.

I am always with you here
while also with the Spirit,
the movement of nature,
and with my own sweet children,
wherever they are.

I am in so many places at one time.

Prompt ~ Where Are You? ☑

Writing + Mindfulness Activity
Tools: Your *Leap Journal*, a pen, timer, plus tools for your chosen activity
Time: 20 minutes

Have you ever had the feeling after a good night's sleep that you had been very busy in your dreams? The mind is an amazing thing. We can be physically in one place while also feeling as if we've visited many others through the power of our imaginations. While there is great power in being fully present and doing one thing at a time, it can also be very interesting to pay attention to where we are traveling in our minds, and to ask ourselves why.

- Make a list of all the places—positive and negative—that your energy has been traveling to in your mind lately.

- Look at your list and circle the one place that is calling to you most, or that you'd like to explore further. (Examples might be wanting to spend more time with a faraway loved one, or devoting time to a creative product.)

- Get all the tools or supplies needed for the place or activity you circled. If it's not something you can do physically, like being with someone far away, you can also do this as a visualization exercise or research project.

- Set a timer for 20 minutes. During that time, focus only on the one activity that you chose. If you find your attention wandering, gently and lovingly bring your attention back the way you might guide a young child.

For the 20 minutes, try to be fully focused and present with what you have chosen. Try to be there completely.

Prompt ~ Your Dream Home ☀

Art Project
Tools: Your *Leap Journal*, a pen, paper, shoebox, and art supplies
Time: 20 minutes

Home is often the foundation of our lives, the place where we are while our creativity takes us to so many other places, even if only in our minds. Home can be like a springboard. The stronger and more rooted we feel in our own home or sense of being, the higher we can go.

In your *Leap Journal*, complete the following sentences:

- To me, home means…
- My ideal home would be…
- I'd love sharing my ideal home with…
- It would be important for my ideal home to have…
- This matters most of all…

What elements from your list does your current home have? What are some steps you can take to nurture a greater sense of love, creativity, acceptance, or anything else you desire into your current living environment? What changes do you want to make?

- Make a small model, collage, or sketch that represents the energy or feelings you would like to experience in your home. You could do this with a simple sketch in your journal or make a diorama with a shoebox, or a collage out of magazine photos.

Prompt ~ Back Home ♥

Writing Exercise
Tools: Your *Leap Journal* and a pen
Time: 10 minutes

Make a list of all the homes in which you have lived. What was it about them that made them feel like home?

Was there anything about them that was less than nurturing or made them not always feel like the home you needed or wanted at the time? What was missing? What was too much? What was just right?

Which was your favorite home? Why? What made it so special? What are some elements of that home that you can bring into your current living space?

> *"Look at your feet. You are standing in the sky. When we think of the sky, we tend to look up, but the sky actually begins at the earth…we breathe it deep within us."*
>
> *~Diane Ackerman*

As I Awake

As I wake,
the sky is plain glass,
a haze across the day.

Or is it my eyes?

I can never tell,
first thing in the morning,
what is my own inner fog
and what is an outer mist.

And so,
I rub my eyes,
pour the coffee,
and ponder these things
as I wake up.

Prompt ~ Morning Gratitude ☑

Life Practice
Tools: A notebook and pen
Time: One week

The power of gratitude can uplift our energy, making us more open to new creative ideas and possibilities. For one week, try this exercise.

- Before going to sleep at night, put a notebook and pen by your bed.
- As soon as you wake up, start making a list of all the things you are grateful for.
- Carry this notebook with you during your morning routine.
- Jot down anything you are thankful for during the day. You might include little things like running water, toothpaste, a cup of coffee, your child's smile, etc.
- At night, return the notebook to your bedside.
- Re-read your list before falling asleep.

> *"The miracle of gratitude is that it shifts your perception to such an extent that it changes the world you see."*
>
> ~Dr. Robert Holden

Locked Away

I bet you're wondering
how to be a dreamer
while still a human
grounded
in this world
of need and tasks
and must-dos.

I am too.

The one thing
I have found
that works for me,
sometimes,
is locking up the poems,
turning away
and saying,
"I'll be back"

And really doing it.

In the best of times
when conditions
are just right,
we return
to discover small seeds
have sprouted
into little tendrils,
reaching out
for our help
with the next step
in their growth.

So we tend
and weed
and feed
and mulch
and till the soil
until life calls us
away again.

The trick is
never going away
too long and
on occasion,
if a magic bean
was planted by mistake
and a vine is growing
or weeds
threatening
to strangle
what you've started,
then for heaven sakes,
lock up your life instead.

For life too
can take its turn
sometimes

And wait.

Prompt ~ Breadcrumb Trail ☑

Writing Exercise + Life Practice
Tools: Your *Leap Journal*, a pen, plus tools related your chosen goal
Time: 20 minutes

I often feel as if I am juggling many different projects and priorities. When I put one down for too long, sometimes I find it difficult to get back into it, or to remember where I left off.

In the fairy tale, *Hansel and Gretel*, Hansel left a trail of breadcrumbs through the forest so later he and his sister could follow them back to find their way home again. This prompt is about brainstorming what can act as a trail of breadcrumbs, helping you find your way back to projects that you'd really like to complete, or priorities you haven't focused on in a while. Examples of breadcrumbs might include leaving yourself notes, setting out your supplies before you take a break, etc.

Complete the following sentences in your *Leap Journal*.

- A priority I want to put more focus on is…
- This is important to me because…
- A project I really want to complete is…
- After it's completed, here's how my life might change…
- I often get distracted by…
- These things get in my way…
- These things make it hard to remember where I left off…

- I would have a higher chance of completing this task if…
- I would do this activity more often if…
- Something that's even more important is…
- Here's how I could nurture and protect both…
- After I complete this project, I will feel…
- What matters most is…
- Here are a few changes that might help me to focus more on my top priorities…

Today, spend 20 minutes doing something to help get yourself organized, get your supplies ready, make a list, etc., so you will be in a better position to focus on and complete what matters most to *you*.

> *"Your vision will become clear only when you look into your heart. Who looks outside, dreams; who looks inside, awakes."*
>
> *~Carl Jung*

In Between

It might go away,
this way I have of writing,
thinking in prose,
tucking a poem
in between
coffee and a shower.

But for now,
it suits me
as I haven't time
for anything else.

Prompt ~ On the Hour ☀

Music and Movement
Tools: A timer
Time: One day

When life feels overwhelming or we are going through a challenging time, it can be helpful to come up with little tricks to keep our energy high. For this prompt, we are going to practice the power of taking mini breaks to stay uplifted.

- Set a timer to go off every hour.

- Each time your timer goes off, spend one minute walking and moving your body while humming an uplifting, catchy song.

Your walks can be as simple as walking to the restroom, walking from one area of your home or office to another, or even around the block, or out to your mailbox and back again.

Your chosen song might be something like *Don't Worry, Be Happy* (Bob Marley), *Zip-a-dee-doo-da* (Song of the South), *What a Beautiful Morning* (South Pacific), *Don't Worry, Be Happy* (by Bob Marley), *Up, Up with People* (Sing It Out Musical), etc. Choose a positive song that means something special to you. If you are in a public place, you can also just imagine singing the song in your mind.

- As the day goes on, try swapping out the lyrics with your own. Change the words around. Write your own version.

In addition to staying positive, this is also a fun way to stay connected to your creative voice.

> *"Life is a series of natural and spontaneous changes. Don't resist them-that only creates sorrow. Let reality be reality. Let things flow naturally forward in whatever way they like."*
>
> ~Lao-Tse

The Puppy

She watches me,
my every move

Waiting to see
where I will go next.

Is this the way
Devotion works?

Tracking, hovering,
staying close

To receive
the Offering

Whatever it may be.

Maybe this is true love.

Or perhaps it is simply
what the Devoted do
when they are following
their Master.

As for me,
I think she came to teach me
what I need to do about
Inspiration.

Stay close.

Track it with all your senses.
Smell. Sight. Hearing.

And when it moves,
follow it and see what happens.

Prompt ~ True Devotion ☑

Writing Exercise
Tools: A timer, Your *Leap Journal*, and a pen
Time: One day

What are some ways you can nurture your relationship with your creativity, the way you would a new romance?

Can the puppy's strategy help?

Stay close.
Track it with all your senses.
...And when it moves, follow it and see what happens.

Set a timer for seven minutes and brainstorm some creative ways you can be more devoted and loyal to your creative gifts. Write down your insights.

> "*Knowledge does not come to us by details, but in flashes of light from heaven.*"
>
> *~Henry David Thoreau*

I Smile

I smile,
resting now
after a long hard day of work.

We weeded and swept
and packed and cleared.

Decluttering time.

Summer clean-up.

Getting things done.

It takes so long to get here.

But when the work is finished
and we can lean back in sunlight
and relax without guilt

It feels so settled.

So good.
So calm.

Rest well-earned.
Tall cool drink with ice in glass.

It's good to remember
when I don't want to lift a finger
what this feels like.

After the working is done

Rest is different.

Prompt ~ Clean a Junk Drawer ☑

Life Practice
Tools: A timer and clutter
Time: 20 minutes

Completing tasks is incredibly beneficial to our sense of accomplishment, energy levels, and confidence. It also trains our brain to focus, which can help us get us into flow, and boost our intuition and creativity.

Find a small corner of your home that needs your attention. Set aside 20 minutes to clean it. You might choose a junk drawer, your refrigerator, a shelf in your closet, or your email inbox. Make sure you choose a decluttering job that you can complete in 20 minutes.

It's amazing how little spurts of clearing and cleaning can boost our moods and energetically create space in our psyches and our lives. The more we let go of those things that no longer support where we want our lives to go, the more we gain energy to follow where our creative voice is calling us *next.*

"*Every hour of the light and dark is a miracle.*"

~Walt Whitman

Dress Rescue

Finding the dress,
pulling it out
of old trash bag
destined for
the donation box and

Saving Its Life.

Prompt ~ Display a Treasure ☑

Life Practice + Writing Exercise
Tools: A timer, your home, your *Leap Journal*, and a pen
Time: 10 minutes to one hour

The sense that we are missing out on something, are lacking, or that we *need* something *out there* can be very draining and distracting. For this prompt, we are going to train our brains to remember how much we already have by searching for treasures in our homes.

Look through your home for something that makes you smile. It might be something old and forgotten, or even tucked into a junk drawer. It might be something you love simply because of its color or shape.

If it's an article of clothing, what's a new way you can wear it? If it's an object, create a special place for it in your home, perhaps by displaying it on an altar, special table, or by putting it in a frame. Honor how special it is to you and how happy it makes you feel.

- Find new ways to expand the energy of this treasure in your life, regardless of how simple or unimportant it may seem to others.

In your *Leap Journal*, complete the following sentences. (If you don't know the real story, imagine what the answers to these questions *might* be.)

- The story behind my treasure is…
- It is special because…
- It represents…

- Its message is…
- Similar forgotten treasures I have are…
- What I treasure most of all is…

> *"We can only be said to be alive in those moments when our hearts are conscious of our treasures."*
>
> *~Thornton Wilder*

Waiting for Words

She lays there
in the sunlight

Quietly waiting
for her girl
to come back.

For I am too boring
as I write.

She knows it's important, though

Because she has abandoned
her ball and toy,
even stopped begging
for a treat
or second helping
just to make the time pass.

Her ears perk
as the silent house groans,
settling
clicking
with the hum of electronics
that run themselves.

Could it be her boy waking?

Then she decides it's not
and plops back down
waiting for me to stop
my endless
writing
so we can
play.

Prompt ~ Waiting Patiently ☑

Writing Exercise + Life Practice
Tools: A timer, your home, your *Leap Journal*, and a pen
Time: Five minutes + one week

We all know how it feels like to wait after sending an email, invitation, text, or message before hearing the other person's reply. It can be difficult to wait, especially if we feel as if what we are waiting for is required to move our lives to the next stage.

In your *Leap Journal*, complete the following sentences:

- I am waiting for...
- Some creative ways I can use this time are...
- Something that would uplift me as I wait is...
- I can still move this project ahead in a positive way by...
- I can prepare for what's next by...

For example, you could listen to a podcast, explore another lead or idea, meet with a friend to brainstorm next steps, go for a nature walk, clean your house, plant a garden, start meditating, do something fun or whimsical, etc. We can keep our creative energy flowing even when the outside world pauses. Try one of your ideas this week.

> "*An unhurried sense of time is in itself a form of wealth.*"
>
> ~*Bonnie Friedman*

Awe

When I was young
I used to love to wake up early
and watch the sunrise,
ribbons in the sky.

I'd sneak out of the house and
gaze at the beams of light
striking a baseball field
near our home.

Pure magic.

I forgot how

Awe

makes everything Right.

Prompt ~ Pure Magic ☀

Writing Exercise
Tools: Your *Leap Journal* and a pen
Time: 20 minutes

What is something in your life that you experience as perfect, just as it is? It might be a favorite possession, dessert, meal, a routine, relationship, flower, season, scent, candle, perfume, or something in nature you often notice.

- Write a poem or paragraph describing it to someone who has never experienced this thing in your life that to you is "pure magic."

Don't worry about the quality of your writing. Focus on really describing what this thing is, and why it is so magical to you personally. Include words that engage all the senses, like how it looks, smells, sounds, looks, feels, etc.

> *"We are all dreaming of some magical rose garden over the horizon – instead of enjoying the roses that are blooming outside our windows today."*
>
> *~Dale Carnegie*

Memoir

My memoir
began
the day
I stopped
doing

and started

listening

and

writing

what I heard.

Prompt ~ Revelation ☀

Writing Exercise
Tools: Your *Leap Journal* and a pen
Time: 20 minutes

One of the most effective ways to learn how we want to live our lives is through the power of stories. Most stories have a moment of crisis where the protagonist needs to determine whether something is right for him or her personally. The character might come up against strong resistance or guidance from people who are supposed to know better.

You can use this prompt to uncover your own personal formula for creating a turnaround.

Part 1

Think of a movie, novel, or well-known story where the main character had a decision to make, and ultimately chose a path that was right for him or her that turned everything around. Some examples include *Moana, Little Red Riding Hood, Scooby Doo, Anne of Green Gables, Rocky, Spiderman, The Black Panther, Harry Potter*, or real-life events in the lives of individuals like Martin Luther King, Jr., Gandhi, Rosa Parks, Susan B. Anthony, George Washington, Abraham Lincoln, Buddha, Jesus, John the Baptist, Moses, etc.

- Write down the steps the main character took to help this turnaround happen. Describe the moment when they realized that what they were doing was working.

Part 2

Now think of a turnaround moment in your own life. It might be as simple as you were losing a game, but then something happened and you won instead, or something more profound like overcoming depression, recovering from an illness, or meeting your partner.

- Describe the moment when you knew that what you were doing was helping.
- How would you describe your turnaround formula to others?
- How is it different or the same as what worked in the story in Part 1?
- Is there anything you learned that you can apply to a current situation in your life?

Write down any insights you gain from this exercise in your *Leap Journal*.

> *"Straightaway the ideas flow in upon me, directly from God."*
>
> ~*Johannes Brahms*

Plums and Apricots

Plums and apricots
Juice overflowing
Dripping down my hand

Abundance wasted
So hard to keep up
With the overflow

of Harvests.

Prompt ~ Receiving Abundance ☀

Art Project
Tools: Paper, old magazines, items from nature, crayons, glue, or tape
Time: One hour

- What are some things in your life that make you feel abundant, that you would love to freeze in time so you could access them whenever you'd like? They might include the feeling of holding a loved one's hand, a favorite food, the smell of your favorite season, etc.

Create a collage or display that includes these favorite items. This can include photos from a magazine, pictures you draw, or actual items from nature, etc. Display your abundance collage or collection in a place you see often.

> *"The breeze of grace is always blowing on you, but you have to unfurl your sails."*
>
> *~Sri Ramakrishna*

Oops, I Forgot

Yesterday was the day
we were going to celebrate
life itself.

Oops, I forgot.

Prompt ~ Plan a Celebration 

Art Project
Tools: Your *Leap Journal*, a pen, and supplies needed for your celebration
Time: 20 minutes to multiple days

If you were to plan a celebration of all the things you love most about your life, what would that be like?

- Would you invite others, or have it just for yourself or a few close loved ones?
- Where would you host the celebration?
- What would the color scheme be?
- What would the invitations be like?
- How would you decorate?
- Would you say any words, have any music, or a special ceremony?

Write it all down. Plan an imaginary party (or a real one!) to honor what is most special and what you are most grateful for in your life.

> "*Take as a gift whatever this day brings forth.*"
>
> ~*Horace*

Self-Reflection

~Living Your Creative Life~

We are often so busy living our lives that we don't realize that there is a rhythm and art to how we live. It can be helpful to look at our lives through the lens of a loving witness with the rare ability to see the magic in the mundane. Shifting our ideas about how our lives are supposed to work can offer clarity about how we can get our lives flowing again.

Write your answers to the following questions in your *Leap Journal.*

- How does your current life make you feel?
- What do you love most about your life?
- What do you like least about your life?
- Are there any quirks or ways you have of doing things that someone who was falling in love with you might find particularly endearing?
- If there were a theme song describing your life, what might it be?
- If you were able to change the vibe of your life, what would you want it to be like?
- What do you wish would never change about your life?

What's Your Leap?

What's one simple way you can bring more joy into your everyday life?

Circles

Who uplifts you?

I remember waking before sunrise and hearing my father pacing on the living room floor in his pajamas, whispering under his breath as he practiced his sermon on Sunday mornings. Occasionally he would pause to make a quick handwritten edit in the margin of the legal pad filled with his notes as he paced, back and forth, not realizing I was watching.

The mornings when I had the rare privilege to witness him at work molded me. When I was in high school, my English teacher once asked me where I had learned to write. Not knowing quite how to answer, I faltered, then blurted out: "My father is a writer."

The truth was that my father was a Presbyterian minister. The fact that he was a preacher, and my siblings and I were PKs (preacher's kids) was something I typically hid from those who didn't already know, mostly out of self-protection. Once they heard what he did for a living, they would inevitably make assumptions about who I was, what I believed, and who he was, thinking they had us all figured out based on their own personal experiences with religion.

We all do this, of course, making sense of the world and each other based on the few details we have. We all have the desire to be known for who we really are in a world that is quick to judge, sharing their own version of our identity as truth, as well as what it *means*.

Our desire to be known and seen becomes even more complicated when we are still figuring it out for ourselves. Most of us don't want to be told who we are, we want to discover it, in our own time and space, in our own way.

The truth is, regardless of how he was known by the outer world, he was first and foremost my dad, and then a writer and poet, someone who knew firsthand the ups and downs of striving to honor the soft, still voice within. He understood the struggle of wanting to get to the truth, both on paper and in how he lived his life, which was constantly bulging with complications. By quietly watching him, I learned about the struggle to be true to oneself, opening to creative fragments, and the art of paying attention.

I now realize my experience with my father was not all that unique. Whether it's our own families, close friends, or other creators sharing their work with the world, we are all surrounded by a circle of creative support that we can tap into on our journey of living in alignment with who we really are. Although it may look different for each of us, we are constantly being offered teachers, guides, mentors, and sources of support that show us how to live more inspired, authentic lives, whether these teachers come in the form of loved ones or the energy of people we don't even know. Often the only thing we need to do to tap into this greater wisdom and become uplifted is to open to receiving gifts from unexpected people and places.

Our circles can be filled with creative and intuitive friends, teachers, coaches, or simply fellow creators who have persevered and found their own way. With a simple nod or understanding glance, we know they get it—the inner journey of going past gremlins and clutter to get to our truth. Just as often, our circles are formed through names on the covers of books, characters in movies, singers and songwriters, or by witnessing the beauty of another's life from a distance. Our circles can include anyone whom we've known personally or have admired, making us feel less alone in our struggles to discover and be known for who we really are, and to express the creative, intuitive yearnings within our own hearts.

Our circle of support may not seem like anything out of the ordinary—friends, family members, or acquaintances who come and go, showing up at just the right moment when we need a comforting glance or shoulder to lean on, or a contrarian perspective that we may disagree with to this day, but that was just the thing our art or life needed, like pepper in a bland dish.

A creative circle is made up of those who are willing to dive deep when the dark underworld is what is needed to understand now. Within our circle are those who think creatively and those who are deeply committed to following their own intuition. If they aren't creating themselves, then they often have their ear in someone else's music, or their nose in someone else's book. Most of all, they tend to be comfortable enough with uncertainty and their own dark places that they accept us just as we are when we are battling with our own.

Supportive friends know what it means to get triggered, to battle with feelings of inadequacy and self-doubt, to be human and share our imperfections out in the open on paper or on canvas, to take leaps that make us feel vulnerable. They know what it's like to live in a state of soaking up wisdom and small details for no other reason than it completes the puzzle of life. We need people in our lives who are in the thick of their own creative, intuitive processes and generous enough to hold space for us to admit our own. They remind us we are not alone, whether simply by how they live, or making us laugh out loud.

In the absence of real human bodies, any writer who writes about writing, artist who shares her process, therapist or healer who offers support from the place of their own healing, or athletes, actors, or personalities who share a glimpse into their inner victories can play the part of holding us in that sacred space from which our own creativity and intuition can grow.

Some of my most complicated and deepest relationships have been with other creators. They are the ones who even after decades of being apart, whether our relationship ended on an up or a down, can with a glance remind us of who we really are, or who we once were. In our darkness moments, it is our truest of friends, lovers, fathers, mothers, sisters, brothers, healers, way showers, teachers, and fellow creators who make us smile and keep us real—they are the pedestal on which each detail of our art stands.

We are all being supported by a circle of support, even if an invisible one. Our circle may include voices from past generations, whispers from our future, people who have loved and seen us, offering the right word or acknowledgement when we thought we were invisible. Others in our circle may have wounded us, etching on our hearts' indelible resilience, wisdom, empathy, and insight to be woven into artistry for generations to come. We are important members of this circle too, often providing just what another creator, visionary, or friend most needs without even realizing it.

Without this circle of support in whatever form it takes, surrounding us in each day and our memories, our creative work and lives would be oh, so different.

> "*...As we let our own light shine, we unconsciously give other people permission to do the same.*"
>
> *~Marianne Williamson*

I Suspect He Knew

The one thing
I think is a shame
is that he didn't know me
as a poet.

For if he had,
we could have had a chat
about the index cards
he kept tucked
in his front pocket,
pen close by.

And we could have had a laugh
about whether they were
all really
to-do lists
and people's names,
important facts and figures.

Or whether an
occasional phrase
that hovered
between the now
got through.

I only wish
I had started
writing poetry
when he was here.

Somehow,
I suspect,
even if it wasn't
happening to me
yet
and my writing was different than his

Somehow,
I suspect
he knew.

Prompt ~ What Didn't You Say? ♥

Writing Exercise
Tools: Your *Leap Journal* and a pen
Time: 10 minutes

Unfinished business often distracts us, keeping us from being present and recognizing new opportunities. Is there someone who is no longer in your life, whom you often think about? Answer the following questions in your *Leap Journal*:

- What's something you didn't have a chance to tell them before they left your life, or your relationship changed in some way?
- Is it possible to share this with them even now? (Perhaps by writing a letter, or calling them on the phone, etc.)
- If it is not possible or not in your best interest to reach out to them directly, close your eyes for a moment. Imagine telling them in your imagination.
- How do you feel after doing this? Write it down.

> *"Belonging…doesn't require us to change who we are; it requires us to be who we are."*
>
> *~Brené Brown*

Eggs and My Reader

I never knew
how important
it was
to have my words
received.

This is what I am thinking about
as I separate eggs.

Two halves of the shell,
cups in which I
pour the yolk
back and forth,
a game of catch
from one to the next
as the white drips
a harvest into my bowl.

One reader,
one life,
one open hand and heart
receiving what I offer
taking it from me,
completing the chain,
carrying it
into her own life
and consciousness.

Spreading how
I don't know
and never will
for now
it is
no longer mine.

For each reader who takes the time
to pause upon a word,
I am grateful.

Because it lifts a weight.

Words like letters sent
need to be opened,
cycle not complete
until unsealed.

Just as I reread and edit,
taking in
what I thought I meant
and discover
more in my own words
than I ever knew.

This is what I am thinking
as the egg whites
for my daughter
sizzle in their pan.

Prompt ~ Mindful Connections ☀

Mindfulness Activity
Tools: Other people in your space
Time: 3 minutes

Find a space where you can spend a few minutes in silence that includes other people. You could do this exercise in a coffee shop, a restaurant, store, or in your own home with your family.

This prompt is designed to help us stay open to others while also letting go of preconceived notions about our own roles. You can do this exercise with your eyes open or closed. Without interrupting or distracting the other people nearby, focus your attention on one of them. What do you notice about them intuitively?

- How do you think they are feeling?
- What is their energy like?
- What are they communicating without any words?
- What do you appreciate about them?
- Practice accepting them without trying to figure out, fix, or help.
- Imagine sending them accepting, loving energy.

After completing this exercise, assess how you feel.

- How do you feel about them and the world?
- How do you feel about yourself?

Prompt ~ Being of Service ☑

Writing Exercise
Tools: Your *Leap Journal* and a pen
Time: 10 minutes

We all have moments when our lives become about something bigger than ourselves. We may start doing an activity simply because it brings us joy, then become aware of an inner passion to do it in a way that will also help others.

It's important to remember that our ability to help ourselves is directly related to our ability to help others. Answer the following questions in your *Leap Journal*:

- What is something you would love to do to help others?

Complete the following sentences:

- I want to help others to...
- I want to help myself to...
- A unique perspective I have to offer is...
- I can help myself and others most by...

> *"Let no one ever come to you without leaving better and happier. Be the living expression of God's kindness: kindness in your face, kindness in your eyes, kindness in your smile."*
>
> ~Mother Teresa

Friends

There have been friends
who crossed my path
as quickly as I theirs

And yet their
footprints
are those I walk in when lost

Their backs
are those
I lean against
when weak

Their eyes
still light my path
so I can find my way.

So brief,
so fleeting
were our meetings
to last forever.

There are friends
whose connection
travels with us
even when we have lost touch.

They are the
perfect color,
the just-right hue
in which to dip
our brush

when looking for that
one thing
that will serve that purpose,
fill that gap,
an empty space.

Even now,
they fit us
so perfectly
that for one moment,
one point in time,
they fill us up,
making it all right.

They remain with us always,
if only in a memory.

These are the friends
who are in our lives forever.

Prompt ~ Thank You Note ☀

Writing Exercise
Tools: Writing paper or a thank you card, pen, envelope, and stamp
Time: 20 minutes

When we appreciate others, this doesn't just benefit the recipients, it also blesses us. Gratitude opens our hearts and can lead to amazing synchronicities and opportunities.

- Write a thank you note to a friend, saying thanks for all the things they have done for you.

- You might even give yourself a 28-day thank you note writing challenge and write one note a day to those who have made a real difference in your life.

You might send your thank you notes to loved ones, friends you've have lost contact with, writers, teachers, artists, or musicians whose creative works have touched you in a deep way or have changed your life.

See if the energy shifts between you and these individuals even before you send your letters.

Prompt ~ True Friends ☑

Writing Exercise
Tools: Your *Leap Journal* and a pen
Time: 20 minutes

We are constantly evolving, and so are the people in our lives. When we are aware of what we need, want, and what we are willing to offer others, new friendships often miraculously appear. Self-awareness can help our existing relationships evolve and change form too. Answer the following questions in your *Leap Journal*.

- If you could design the perfect friend, what would they be like?
- What would you feel like when you were with them?
- What role would you want them to play in your life?
- What role would you like to play in theirs?
- Does your description remind you of anyone you know? Where do you think someone like that might spend their time?

Next, describe the type of friend that you are:

- How do you think you make other people feel? What unique gifts and energy do you have to offer?
- Do you have any relationships you would like to deepen?
- What's something you can do to experience more joy with others?
- What kind of new friendships would you like to attract?

Prompt ~ Finding Time ☑

Writing Exercise + Art Project
Tools: Your *Leap Journal*, colored pencils, and a pen
Time: 10 minutes

When we are busy, we often live our lives on automatic pilot. Every now and then, it can be helpful to assess whether the choices we are making are helping or hindering us in taking more creative leaps.

- Make a pie chart approximating how much time you spend with each person in your life including time spent alone.

You might put down 20% for your partner or kids, 40% for people at work, or 50% for time alone, etc. Be sure to date your pie chart, as how we spend our time often changes.

- Now take some time to assess how being with each person on your pie chart makes you feel. You might want to color each according to the spectrum of the rainbow: Red-Orange-Yellow-Green-Blue-Indigo-Violet (ROYGBIV), with red being the most complicated of emotions, and purple being the most positive. Here are some ideas on how this can work.

Uplifted = Purple: If you almost always feel happy or peaceful with someone, or as if you are truly seen and appreciated, color their piece of pie purple/violet.

Positively Connected = Indigo: If you feel a positive, intuitive connection with someone, color their piece of the pie indigo.

Positive Potential = Light Blue: If you usually have positive experiences with someone but feel as if your connection could go deeper, color their section light blue.

Unbalanced = Green: If you usually feel positive with someone but feel as if your exchanges are often unequal, choose green.

Competitive = Yellow: If you often feel on guard with someone, as if they are competing with you, or as if they are undermining you in some way, color their piece of the pie yellow.

Drained = Orange: If you frequently feel drained after spending time with someone, color their section orange.

Toxic = Red: If you almost always get triggered by someone, or feel as if they are subtly or directly attacking you in some way, or if they make you feel unsafe, color their piece of the pie red.

After completing this project, assess what your chart looks like.

- Are there any changes you would like to make to how you spend your time?
- Are there any relationships you would like to take proactive steps to improve? What could you do differently to change the color of a relationship on your chart?
- Are there any people on your chart with whom you would like to spend more time?
- Are there any people on your chart with whom you would like to set better boundaries? Are there requests you'd like to make or relationships you'd like to end?
- Is there any space on your pie chart for someone new?

After you complete your pie chart, review it. Which colors show up the most? What changes can you make so that you feel as positive and peaceful as possible most of the time? Write it all down in your *Leap Journal*.

> "A friend is a present you give yourself."
>
> ~Robert Louis Stevenson

The Red Dress

She shines
like a bolt
of brightness
against the
plain, dull
desert.

An explosion of color.

Artistry
shows up in ways
we least expect
everywhere.

A bud burst

Just because
she chose
the red dress
today.

Prompt ~ Colorful Living ☀

Life Practice
Tools: Your wardrobe
Time: 20 minutes

We are constantly sending out energy, visible and invisible, that tells others how we are feeling and who we are. Color is a concrete, playful way we can experiment with this idea. There is a strong connection between color and emotion.

Look at your wardrobe.

- Which colors do you wear most often?
- Which colors are missing, or don't you wear that often?
- Which colors make you feel happy?

Choose one color you rarely wear but like, and find a way to add it to your life. You might choose something in this new color that you already own but rarely wear or buy yourself something new. (It can be something simple like a scarf, hat, or new t-shirt.) You might also buy something for your home in this color, like a bouquet of flowers or a throw pillow. See how you feel and how your energy shifts when you make space for this color in your life.

> *"And the day came when the risk to remain tight in the bud was more painful than the risk it took to blossom."*
>
> *~Anais Nin*

Drips of Me

What I like
about poetry
is that I can share
drips and drops

Just enough
to be caught
in open palm
cupped to catch
what is offered
before it disappears.

In this way,
I can share
my deepest being
with those I love,
a little
at a time
without taking up
too
much
space.

Prompt ~ Mini Me ☀

Writing Exercise + Art Project
Tools: Your *Leap Journal,* a pen, and colored pencils
Time: 20 minutes

Life can be so busy, many of us find ourselves fitting genuine connections with others into little slivers of time through texts, distracted conversations, or short FaceTime calls. A common marketing tactic is called the "elevator speech." The idea is to develop a memorized description of your product, service, identity, or business that you could deliver in the amount of time you would have with someone on an elevator.

For this prompt, we are going to use the power of brevity to get greater clarity about who we are, our unique energy, gifts, what matters most to us, and how we would like to connect with others.

Option 1 ~ True Self Elevator Speech

In your *Leap Journal*, write the following:

- How are you feeling in this moment?
- What unique gifts do you have that you'd like to share?
- If your True Self had one message, what might that be?
- What does the energy of your True Self feel like?
- If your True Self had a unique gift to offer, how might you describe it? Can you describe it in just one sentence? In three words? One word?

Prompt ~ True Self Logo ☀

Writing Exercise + Art Project
Tools: Your *Leap Journal*, a pen, and colored pencils
Time: 20 minutes

Logos are another simple marketing technique used to communicate something's essence. Logos are so effective because they communicate ideas the way our unconscious minds process information, which is through symbols.

- What is a symbol that represents what matters most to you?
- What colors or symbols represent the energy of your True Self?
- What is a symbol that represents a leap you want to take?
- How do you want your life to feel?
- How could you incorporate these into your own personal logo?

Have fun with this. Experiment. Let your logo be imperfect. You don't ever have to show your logo to others (unless you want to!). Instead, this is a great way to get clarity and to distill what is most important, the unique gifts you have to offer, and what you value from all of who you are.

- What is important to you about you?

> *"Drop by drop is the pitcher filled."*
>
> *~Buddha*

Way Shower

Thank you, I whisper.
It feels odd to be talking to the dead.

Although I must,
after what happened last night

It would be strange
to not acknowledge it.

Or not to say your name.

Amelia.

I awoke with a start

Full moon
shining brightness
through the cracks in the drapes.

Not knowing what woke me,
exactly,
or why

I just knew I had to
get up.

The time on the clock was 1:11.

I slipped on my slippers
and plodded out
to the living room,

trying my best
to be quiet,
to let my family sleep.

The whole house was lit up
blinds high
moonlight
flooding rooms
as if by LED.

And I did what anyone would do,
I turned on my phone
to catch up on social media.

Somehow, I stumbled
into messages
never opened,
long forgotten.
(I never was very good at this stuff.)

And you sent me one, didn't you?
Eleven years before
when you were still here.

It waited there unopened,
with a link that still worked
to a video I had never played.

A video with the exact answer to what was
happening in my writing
at this exact point in time,
11 years later.

Maybe I wasn't ready
or didn't need the answer as much then
as I do now.

"You might want to think of your
writing like this,"
you had texted,
magical sprite that you are,
whispering to me through the night
from the other side,
wherever that may be.

You shared a link,
and when I clicked,
it led me to
Elizabeth Gilbert
who mentioned
"magical divine entities"
who
"invisibly assist us with our work."

You understood.

Fellow writer,
one of the very few
who understood me,
one of the very few who knew
my torment and delight.

You were in on it,
my sole accomplice.

Why I thought to ask for your help,
then a friend lost touch
and
how we found each other again,
I don't remember.

And yet, you came back last night.

Again.

Didn't you?

As if again you heard
my simple ask,
my task,
the one I had to complete.

You appeared out of nowhere
to help
on my blinking screen.

There are "way showers"
you had written
so long ago
"folks that show you the way who
may or may not stick around..."

Was that foreshadowing?

Why did you have to die so young?

We could have finished the conversation
we started
departed
from each other
then found again.

Oh, that's right.
I get it.
We are.

Right now,
we are having this conversation.
Aren't we?

Really?

Well, then, Amelia,
my Way Shower:

Thanks.

What else can one say
in times like this
when a gift
goes so far beyond
what one can
repay?

Thanks for
showing me
the way
and being
a true friend
long
past
the
end.

Prompt ~ Back in Time 

Writing Exercise + Meditation
Tools: Your *Leap Journal*, a pen, and a private space
Time: 20 minutes

Relationships are how we figure out who we really are and the unique gifts that we have to offer. Sometimes we don't have direct access to people who might be able to help us most of all, such as famous teachers, busy mentors, or loved ones who have passed on.

Who is someone with whom you wish you could have a conversation? Answer these questions in your *Leap Journal*:

- What would you talk about?
- What would you want to tell them?
- What would you like to ask?
- What advice would you seek?
- What gift or guidance would you hope this person might offer you?
- What do you think you might learn?
- What might disappoint you about the conversation?
- What gifts might you offer the other person during the conversation?
- How would a conversation like this make you feel?
- What might change in your life after having this conversation?

- In what way was this person beautifully imperfect and human? In what way was everything that transpired between you when they were alive perfect and beautiful (even if you didn't realize at the time)?

Meditation

Close your eyes, take a few nice deep breaths, and imagine having this conversation now.

You could also write the conversation using your dominant hand to ask this person questions, and your non-dominant hand to record their answers.

After you feel complete, notice how you feel. Record any new insights in your *Leap Journal*.

> *"People will forget what you said, people will forget you did, but people will never forget how you made them feel."*
>
> *~Maya Angelou*

Growing Up

I think I'd like to focus
on how we are different.

How would that be?

Because there's always
so much pressure
to be alike.

Prompt ~ Differences Bond Us ♥

Writing Exercise
Tools: Your *Leap Journal* and a pen
Time: 10 minutes

The more balanced our relationships are, the more easily our lives flow. If we constantly feel as if we are spending a lot of energy supporting others and not getting the support we need, we might notice that our creativity or connection with our inner voice may suffer. Similarly, if we are in a relationship where we are always at ideological odds, we might feel drained. On the other hand, if all our relationships and friendships are with people just like us, we might feel uninspired or not stretch as high as our souls want us to go.

- Make a list of 10 of your favorite people.
- Write next to each name three positive qualities they have that you don't have, at least not quite as much.
- Now go back through your list and write down three positive qualities you have that they don't have as much.
- Look back over your list. Are you more different or alike?
- To what extent do you balance each other?
- What do you have to offer the relationship?
- What are you grateful to the other person for?
- How could this relationship continue to help you grow?

Record any insights you have in your *Leap Journal*.

Prompt ~ Nothing to Fix ♥

Mindfulness Activity
Tools: Yourself, friends and family members, and your *Leap Journal*
Time: One week

Many years ago, I was asked to facilitate a women's circle of about 25 women. Originally, I suggested that after each person shared, we all would simply sit in silence for a moment to help us really be present and hear what was being said without offering any advice. A few of the participants protested, expressing that one of the things they like most about their relationships with other women is the give and take of advice.

We agreed on a compromise. It would be up to the person sharing to ask for what she wanted, whether it was just to be heard, feedback, or ideas. We also agreed that before offering any advice or feedback, even if requested, we would each try to pause and tune into our own feelings, to be as clear as possible about any unconscious desire we might have to "fix" the other person, their situation, emotions, or about how our advice would be received.

Often our yearning to give others advice comes from a real heartfelt place of wanting to help and be of service. But offering advice can also serve other purposes that have more to do with us than the other person. For example, giving others advice can help us explore how a solution we have been experimenting with in our own lives can apply to our friend's situation, which may or may not be helpful to them.

Other times, giving advice can be a knee-jerk response to emotions we may not realize we are feeling. It can be very difficult to witness someone suffering. Offering unsolicited advice, solutions, or trying to fix others with quick answers can be a way of distracting ourselves from our own emotional discomfort or distress, or soothing our own anxiety about what they are experiencing.

We also might be coming from a manipulative position without realizing it. Our desire for them to change their ways might be in part to make our lives easier, rather than us being solely focused on their best interest.

Staying connected to our own truth and emotions while also staying open to others is a skill that can take a lifetime to cultivate, and is something I'm constantly working on in my own life. Our ability to do this can also change depending on how we are being triggered, what we are feeling, and what else is happening in the moment.

In most cases, what is most helpful is simply letting the other person know they have been truly seen and heard, which is something most of us desire. For example, you might try saying something genuine and honest like "that sounds really difficult" or "If I were you, I think that would make me feel nervous." This allows safe space for them to agree or disagree rather than us automatically assuming we know how they are feeling, or what is in their best interest.

Depending on the relationship, it can also be helpful to admit when we are triggered or on automatic pilot, to help ourselves reset or come back to the moment, or to simply pause and breathe. It's important to be open to being wrong, rather than making their story about *us*.

Most times, the greatest service we can provide is by simply listening and letting others have and claim their own insights. People are often far more capable of solving their own challenges and inner dilemmas than we (or they) realize. Mindfully pausing and tuning into whatever is happening in each moment, whether our own or others' feelings, is a skill that can greatly improve our relationships, conserve our energy, help others feel respected, and support them in hearing their own truths.

It can be helpful to remember that everyone is on a different journey. We are all doing the best we can with the unique set of challenges, gifts, and experiences we have been given.

This prompt involves increasing our present-moment awareness of how other people's stories make us feel.

- For the next week, when you are having a conversation or listening to others, notice what emotions are coming up for you. Silently name these emotions in your own mind, like: "sad, mad, glad," etc.

- If you find yourself getting caught up in the details or emotions of another person's story, try to guess how they might be feeling. Silently label in your own mind the emotions the other person seems to be feeling, such as angry, anxious, scared, etc.

- If you find yourself wanting to offer advice, *fix* what they might be experiencing, or change their emotions, take a deep breath. Shift your focus back to yourself. Silently label your *own* emotions again. If it helps, you might silently remind yourself: "I am feeling (insert emotion) and that's okay."

- Even if they have directly requested your advice, go slowly and speak mindfully, keeping your attention on what might be most helpful in the present moment. It might help to make your goal accepting whatever you both are feeling as completely normal and okay.

Take notes in your *Leap Journal* about what happens.

Prompt ~ Balancing our Relationships 

Mindfulness Activity
Tools: Your *Leap Journal* and a pen, and another person
Time: 20 minutes + life practice

Our relationships—be they romantic, family roles, or friendships—have a huge impact on the quality of our lives. When our relationships are rooted in love, support, authenticity, honesty, and mutual respect, our well-being often flourishes, and we tend to feel more confident when it comes to taking positive leaps on our own behalf.

Think of an important relationship in your life and answer the following questions in your *Leap Journal*:

- Are you both equally committed to the relationship, and to taking responsibility for the health of the relationship? What are the expectations (direct or unspoken)?

- Do you both feel safe and respected? What are the rules (whether acknowledged or not)?

- Are you each equally respectful and appreciative of the gifts offered by the other? Are there any power imbalances?

- What changes could you make to help the relationship feel more balanced, whether new ways to look out for your own well-being, or new ways to show the other person you value them?

- Is there anything you would like to request that might boost your creativity, or mental, physical, or emotional well-being?

If it feels right, discuss your answers with the other person, or with a trusted healing professional.

Prompt ~ The Art of Repair ♥

Life Practice
Tools: Yourself
Time: One week

Inevitably, at some point or another, our relationships will experience conflict. Humans are not perfect, and our relationships aren't either. We all get triggered and say things or do things on a bad day, that on a good day we wouldn't.

Relationships are like a dance. When we do have a conflict, if the relationship is to continue to be a source of positive support for both people, at some point, both need to actively participate in the repair process.

Some ways we can work towards repair after a conflict include:

- Really hearing what the other person is saying
- Honestly expressing how we are feeling in the moment (I…)
- Seeing the conflict from the other person's point of view and looking for the honest intention behind less than graceful behaviors (most people are coming from a good place)
- Pausing or stepping away when we feel triggered
- Giving the other person space when they seem to be emotionally triggered
- Reaching out about something unrelated to the conflict, such as talking about the weather or making a joke

- Expressing gratitude and focusing on what is good about the relationship or other person
- Reaching out in a kind gesture or initiating doing something fun
- Being on the lookout—others' gestures of repair are often different than our own, or what we think they should be
- Seeking to understand the other person's priorities
- Taking responsibility for and clearly expressing our own priorities
- Acknowledging or responding when other people have taken a step toward repair
- Accepting when the other person is not interested in repair—we can't do their part for them
- Getting support as needed.

For one week, notice anytime you experience a conflict, even if it's with an acquaintance. Experiment with the above list or your own ideas for helping to participate in the process of repair.

Notice what works for you, and what doesn't. Record insights in your *Leap Journal*.

> "*Our work for peace must begin within the private world of each one of us.*"
>
> *~Dag Hammarskjold*

No Common Ground

I have learned
people are made up of beliefs.

A little of this.
A little of that.

I didn't used to think it was this way.

I thought they were
right or left
front or back
up or down.

And we could hang out in a throng
happy together,
all the same.

Now I know we are like a tapestry,
each string a different hue,

Each thought leading to a
checkerboard
filled with choices beneath which
there is

No Common Ground.

Prompt ~ Belief Tapestry ♥

Writing Exercise + Art Project
Tools: Your *Leap Journal*, and colored pencils
Time: 20 minutes

Our perspectives are constantly shifting based on the new experiences and people we encounter every day. How we weave life's influences together to create the tapestry of beliefs, ideas, and perspectives that dictate our lives is ultimately of our own making.

This prompt can help us realize that our beliefs are not fixed, nor does one person, ideology, or institution have complete control over how we view reality.

- Write a list of 20 ideas, beliefs, or opinions that you feel strongly about. Your beliefs might be political, social, personal, spiritual, about how to be healthier, how to be a good friend or partner, or just general ideas about life.

- Which beliefs do you feel a sense of loyalty to, as if changing your belief might be "wrong" or a betrayal of someone else?

- Which beliefs feel as if they are ones of your own making?

- Which are those you've integrated from outside sources?

- Which are the beliefs which were sparked by another person's idea, but to which you have added your own flare?

- What is a new belief that might be emerging in your consciousness that you want to explore further?

- After each belief, write down three or more people or sources who may have influenced or, directly or indirectly, supported you in maintaining this way of thinking. They could be teachers, authors, artists, friends, parents, etc. We have all been molded, taught, and influenced by more people than we often realize.

- In your *Leap Journal*, create a colorful sketch, tapestry, or patchwork quilt filled with the names of all the people who have come together to help make you who you are. Use your imagination to create your own design reflecting all the many different influences who have contributed to how you see the world using a kaleidoscope of color and design.

Use your creativity and have fun! Remember, there is no "right" way to do this. Here are a few ideas:

- You might draw a grid, a patchwork of squares. Then, choose a color to represent each belief on your list. Write the names of all the people who have influenced how you see the world, one name per square. Then, color in the squares with the colors associated with the beliefs that each person influenced. See what patterns unfold.

- You could also create a circle for each belief, surrounded by all the names of those who have contributed or played a role in each belief, like a quilt filled with lots of little belief mandalas.

> *"Dance for yourself, if someone understands, good. If not then no matter, go right on doing what you love."*
>
> ~Lois Hurst

Home

When we are
both
creating,
working on
projects
that make us
happy,
that match our
visions
of how we think
life could be,
something changes.

No longer
are we just
going through
motions.

We shift,
and so does the world.

We are home again

Happily

Together.

Prompt ~ Who is Home? ♥

Writing Exercise
Tools: Your *Leap Journal* and a pen
Time: 20 minutes

Have you ever had the feeling when you were with someone that you were home? It might be with a parent, partner, sibling, child, or best friend, or even someone you met only briefly.

Set a timer for 20 minutes and write in your *Leap Journal* about what it felt like to be with that person. What made them feel like home? Was it familiarity, a sense of being fully known or accepted, or something else?

If you can't think of someone who makes you feel that way, imagine what it might be like to be in a relationship with someone who makes you feel at "home."

Describe in your *Leap Journal* what it might feel like to be in that type of relationship. In your vision, what steps would you both be taking to help nurture and sustain this feeling of home and acceptance?

How could you be that person for yourself? What might you need to change (or do more/less of)? What would you keep the same?

Write in your *Leap Journal* anything that comes up for you on this idea of how your relationships (even your relationship with yourself) can affect your sense of feeling grounded, connected, safe, and at home.

> *"Yes, there is a Nirvanah: it is in leading your sheep to a green pasture, and in putting your child to sleep, and in writing the last line of your poem."*
>
> *~Kahlil Gibran*

Soulmate

How is it
when I first
looked in your eyes
and you made me laugh
so hard
I couldn't breathe
I remembered
you?

Prompt ~ Write a Love Letter ♥

Writing Exercise
Tools: Your *Leap Journal* and a pen
Time: 20 minutes

Write a love letter to someone you care about deeply.

- Tell them everything you cherish about them.

- Consider unexpected traits this person may see as their weaknesses, and tell them why these are actually strengths or gifts.

- Include specific examples of how this person has blessed your life.

If this person is still in your life, consider sharing the letter with them or reading it to them aloud.

> *"Make not a bond of love: let it rather be a moving sea between the shores of your souls."*
>
> *~Kahlil Gibran*

My Wish

If I had one wish
before I go

One thing I'd really want
you to know

It would be
that there is magic
in this world

That you can reach
and you can find.

It starts with you
going into you

And letting go
of the rest.

I'd want you to know
within you
are soft blankets,
still waters,
comfort of
the greatest kind.

And that following formulas
from the outside
doesn't make peace happen.

No, you need permission
from yourself,
not rules or advice

Permission to do it
your own way

To let go of the holding,
to drop down into
wordlessness
where you know,
more than anyone else,
how to do it.

For me to give you advice
would be preposterous

Like Jesus
telling God
what to do.

You know all this,
the answers,
the How.

When you've forgotten

My only wish
for you in this life

Is that you remember.

Prompt ~ Letter to the Future ♥

Writing Exercise
Tools: Your *Leap Journal* and a pen
Time: 20 minutes

Write a letter to future generations. It might be to an actual person, like your children or grandchildren. Or it might be a general letter including your insights about life, the type that could be found in a time capsule for people to open years from now.

- What wisdom have you gained in your life?
- How might your life experience help others when facing challenges or suffering?
- What guidance or advice do you want to pass on?
- How would you like those who read this letter to feel?

> *"There is only one of you in all time, this expression is unique, and if you block it, it will never exist through any other medium; and will be lost...*
>
> *It is not your business to determine how good; it is not how it compares with any other expression. It is your business to keep it yours clearly and directly, to keep the channel open."*
>
> *~Martha Graham*

Whisper in the Air

Don't miss me
for I am still here
with you,
in the ethers

A hush
and holding
a light touch,
remembering our love.

Don't miss me
for I will always be with you
holding you in my palm
like our hands held together,
remembering our love.

Don't miss me.
I will be all around you
reflecting back
what we had
truly
and what will be ours forever.

Love like this
never disappears,
it just expands
so it can hold us everywhere.

Now.

Expanding out
radiating around us
entering the air,
the ethers

A felt experience
of all that we are still
and all that we had.

Don't miss me
for I will always be here
holding and loving you,

a Whisper in the Air.

Prompt ~ What Didn't They Know? 

Writing Exercise
Tools: Your *Leap Journal* and a pen
Time: 20 minutes

Write a letter to your loved ones that you would like them to read after your death.

- What is a message you would like your loved ones to know after you are gone?

- How about while you are still here?

- What haven't you told them that you want to make sure they know?

- What would you like to hear from a loved one?

If it feels right, consider making a copy of this letter and sharing it with them now.

Option:

Another way to do this prompt is to write a letter to someone who has already passed away, or who is no longer in your life. Tell them all the things you wish you had said when you still had access to them in person.

Prompt ~ Invisible You ☀

Writing Exercise + Meditation
Tools: A quiet, private place
Time: Five to 30 minutes

Imagine you have the secret ability to be physically with those you love without them knowing it. While they won't be able to see you, hear you, touch you, etc., they can feel the presence of your energy.

- How would you like your loved ones to experience your energy?

For example, you might want them to feel a sense of peace, beauty, calmness, acceptance, love, abundance, miracles, or as if something good is about to happen.

Meditation

Close your eyes, and practice experiencing this energy within yourself now. Imagine this energy expanding and growing so big that it flows out into the world to be enjoyed by others.

> *"The door lies right within yourself."*
>
> *~Rebecca Clark*

Self-Reflection

~Expanding Your Circle~

We are affected by the people with whom we spend most of our time. When we were very young, we didn't have much choice about who that was. As adults, however, the story is very different. Even if our social circle feels predetermined, we always have choice in how authentically, genuinely, and often we show up.

We often have more options than we might realize when it comes to our connections and relationships. We can expand our circles through social media, joining classes, exposing ourselves to others' creative works, or by joining groups or communities of people that inspire us.

It's not just the people with whom we spend our time who make a difference in our lives, but also our own attitude and openness. Our experiences in the circles in which we travel are as much about our relationships with ourselves as they are about the people whom we are with.

Answer the following questions in your *Leap Journal*:

- Who accepts you just as you are (or has at any point in your life)? If you can't think of anyone, describe what type of person might play that role for you? What would it feel like to be with them?

- Who is someone you feel like you can really trust with your hopes and dreams?

- Who is someone who has entrusted you with a secret or their creative hopes and dreams? How have you nurtured that relationship?
- When you feel creatively blocked, who are your go-to people (or books, movies, shows, podcasts, or music) who help you get unstuck?
- If you were to create your own society or group, what kind of people would be in it? What kind of mindset would you be looking for members to have? What would their vibe be?
- What new insights do you have about your personal circle of loved ones, fellow creators, or friends?

What's Your Leap?

What's one step you can take to expand your circle?

Callings

What's calling you?

I pushed my grandmother's wheelchair over the uneven stones on the patio. It was a gorgeous fall day. She was well in her nineties, and I had learned to cherish each moment, never knowing which visit would be our last.

She leaned back and looked up at the bright blue sky and billowing clouds.

"How would you paint that?" she asked me, pointing with her hands, gnarled with arthritis, at the clouds above.

I looked up, amazed as much by the question as by the contrast of the deep blue and white clouds passing overhead.

She moved her hand back and forth, as if she were painting, imagining the challenge of capturing the clouds on canvas.

Just as I opened my mouth, struggling to come up with some polite answer, she started to talk, telling me which brush strokes she would use, and how she would blend the colors, if she had the chance.

My grandmother was painting all the time in her mind. Paint strokes were running through everything she did, brush stroke after brush stroke. When she was a young girl, she loved to draw. Painting, however, was something she started doing after she retired, spending her well-earned savings on oil painting classes. From that time on, painting became the lens through which she interacted with the world.

Once we each start trusting our true inner voice, following our joy, and claiming our passion, it takes over. We begin creating even when we don't know we are, in our imaginations, our inner psyches. We become collectors, capturing ideas and images, saving them away for when we finally find the time to weave them into something new. Even long after our bodies can comply, like my grandmother's, we continue making our art and living our dreams, if only in our imaginations.

Writing, to me, is like this. It's not about pen on paper, it's the way I move in the world. The more we explore our creativity and intuition, the more we start stocking up experiences, pains, and joys, making sense of other people's anguish, and witnessing with a softness and sensitivity that can make us feel more vulnerable, tuned in and available to the madness, beauty, pain, and magic of each day.

We may feel set apart from others; we witness and participate all at the same time. While joyfully laughing at someone's joke, we are also studying how others live. We are soaking it all up, observing so that we can go back, if not today, then decades from now, weaving the fragments of our lives into magic and wisdom, something to touch the hearts of others, but even more so, to heal our own.

Reclaiming ourselves as our True Selves and the many ways we intuitively feel called to express our truth and shine our light help us find our own unique paths to well-being. We move our ideas of what we want to experience and manifest in our lives from wishes into ways of being. We say yes to the feeling we get when we are living in alignment with our truth and becoming one with a greater flow. We can say with clear consciouses that we are writers, poets, artists, painters, dancers, gardeners, nature lovers, friends, teachers, givers, and receivers because our creativity is not just a passing interest. It is core to who we are, and to who we are becoming.

Owning our creativity and intuition confidently is granted by no one except ourselves. It's not about whether we've had anything published or framed, have degrees to follow our name, or our achievements deemed worthy by others. It's about whether we've made space and claimed the gifts that are ours to enjoy.

Claiming the energy of who we really are means accepting that our creative and intuitive yearnings are not simply wants but needs; if our true inner voice is calling us to create, we need to create like we need breath. If our inner voice is calling us to write, we can't imagine not writing; if our inner voice is calling us to rest and grow, we can't imagine not doing that. Going against our own inner flow is like blocking water, closing the dam.

When we give ourselves the gift of honoring where our inner voice is calling us to go, we pass that gift onto others as well, because we shine a light, our energy is bright. Creators are who we are and whom we were born to be. Honoring our creativity is how we honor being made in the image of a greater Creator.

Some paint, some knit, some create beautiful flower arrangements in a sweet vase. Our intuitive, creative choices, all of them, even the most mundane, become that cord that runs through the motions of our lives and connects us to the very core of who we are.

> *"What you love is a sign from your higher self of what you are to do."*
>
> *~Sanaya Roman*

Not a Poet

I didn't know
I was a poet
until it started
happening to me
at age 50.

Maybe
it's not me at all
but some other-worldly poet
borrowing my hand.

All I know is
she likes
pen and paper.

Prompt ~ A New Name ♥

Writing Exercise
Tools: Your *Leap Journal*, pen, and timer
Time: Five to 10 minutes

Sometimes we can have a lot of clarity about our passion or how to use or share our gifts, and other times, we can feel pulled in lots of different directions. Our callings can change over time and are unique to each of us. Our own ideas about our limitations, potential, value, role, responsibilities, and identity can become barriers which we often need to examine and even leap over before we can truly hear where our inner voice is calling us to go.

So much of how we have come to view ourselves has been handed down to us, almost as if by osmosis. This might include how society or our culture views people like us, whether these perceptions are based on our gender, genetic lineage, economic or educational level, how we learn and express ourselves, our personal preferences and choices, or the wishes, expectations, or underlying emotional needs of our families. In many cases, these expectations and identities are wrapped up in our names, which for most of us were chosen based on our parents' mindset as well as what was happening culturally at the time of our birth.

In many spiritual traditions, individuals at the threshold of adulthood are given a new name or choose one for themselves. For this exercise, we are going to reclaim who we are from an inner rather than outer place.

- Set a timer for five minutes. During that time, keep moving your pen, writing a list of creative new names for yourself.

Use words that make you happy. Play around with your favorite parts of your personality, names you've always liked, or ones that express your hopes for yourself. You might want to use words from nature, other languages, borrow from the media or other cultures, or approach this prompt playfully, like choosing a sequence of words that all begin with your favorite letter, like Passionate Princess Penelope or Dancing Dreaming Danielle. There are no right answers. After the timer goes off, read your list, and circle your favorites.

- If no one else had to know, which new name would you choose?

> *"Your calling isn't something that somebody can tell you about. It's what you feel. It's a part of your life force. It's the thing that gives you juice. The thing you are supposed to do. And nobody can tell you what that is. You know it inside yourself."*
>
> *~Oprah Winfrey*

I've Decided Today

I've decided today
that I am walking forward
toward my dreams
because not to
would be close to suicide.

Not in bodily form,
but death of the greatest part
of myself.

I've decided today
that to be proud and strong,
to stand tall
even in the face of
storms ahead
and memories of those behind
requires nothing less than
simple craziness
and sublime courage.

I've decided that when I stop
or pause,
and there are so many moments
like these
when I yearn to,
there is some small part of me
so much wiser
that whispers and beckons
and reminds me of the freedom
that only comes when one is fully part of oneself.

And the bond
with all those who believe
She is lesser
finally shatter,
broken.

I've decided to lift up and connect
with my Source,
that Voice
that forever whispers:

Come dance with me.
Come play my tune.
Be my soulmate.

And together,
in the dark of the night,
we will steal away
and leap among the stars
until the daylight comes
and we can dance together again
on paper.

Prompt ~ I Promise ☀

Writing Exercise
Tools: Your *Leap Journal*, pen, and timer
Time: 20 minutes

When my husband and I got married, like many couples, we wrote our own wedding vows. The process began with a conversation about marriage and what that meant to us, our values and priorities, and our shared dreams for our partnership. From that point, we started writing, crafting, and finetuning the promises we would make to each other.

We also wrote similar vows to our children when they were born. Over time, these vows have helped to guide our marriage, how we parent, and have helped us to stay true to ourselves.

We can do the same thing for our relationships with our True Selves. Take some time to consider the relationship you have with your true inner voice. You might see this as your egoless self, potential, best self, essence, highest self, Inner Light, Inner Creator, Muse, etc. What you call your True Self is not as important as how you feel about the most peaceful aspect of who you are.

Your relationship with your True Self is extremely powerful, filtering out and affecting every other relationship, choice, and aspect of your life.

The following questions can help you brainstorm what to include in a promise to your True Self:

- What is your current relationship with your inner voice?
- What gets in your way of connecting with this part of yourself?

- What would you like your relationship with your True Self to be like?
- What are you willing to do on an ongoing basis to keep your relationship with your True Self strong?
- How could your relationship with your True Self impact others in a positive way?
- What do you want most of all from your True Self?

Write your own personal vow or promise to your True Self in your *Leap Journal*. You might begin with:

- I (insert name) promise to…

> *"The moment you commit and quit holding back, all sorts of unforeseen incidents, meetings, and material assistance will rise up to help you. The simple act of commitment is a powerful magnet for help."*
>
> *~Napoleon Hill*

Captive Freed

When
tides turn
and you become
a victim of your mind,
remember.

You are a writer.

Because
just as suddenly,
equally without notice,
the captive
will be
freed

And it will be time to work.

Prompt ~ Ready to Work ☑

Writing Exercise
Tools: Your *Leap Journal*, pen, and timer
Time: 10 minutes

In any given moment, we can only do our best. The tricky thing is, our best is constantly changing based on our own state of mind, our physical health, responsibilities, and anything happening in our inner and outer worlds, including events beyond our control, like war, politics, and the weather.

The clearer our vision of our own personal priorities and where we want to go in life, or which creative projects are calling to us the loudest, the easier it is to stay on track with our dreams, even when the volume of the outer world gets turned up high.

Answer the following questions in your *Leap Journal*:

- What is a project you are currently working on, or that you'd like to begin that is deeply important to you?
- What about this project brings you joy?
- What do you hope this project will help you accomplish?
- What is the mission of the project?
- What are your hopes and dreams for the role this project will have in the world?
- What is the most natural next step?

"When you are inspired by some great purpose, some extraordinary project, all your thoughts break their bonds, your mind transcends limitations, your consciousness expands in every direction, and you find yourself in a new, great and wonderful world. Dormant forces, faculties and talents become alive, and you discover yourself to be a greater person by far than you ever dreamed yourself to be."

~Patanjali

Nobles and Slaves

I am related
to kings and queens,
noble stock
hailing from
high castles.

Does it matter?

I come from commoner stock,
mere slave
who did your ancestors' bidding.

Who cares so much
about
achievement and titles,
ground owned
and earned.

Is that the sign of
valor and value?

Making a mark
when we are not,
we point and say,
at least I am that.

When will we say

Proudly

I am me.

I don't know
from where I've come, or
where I'm going, or
whether they'll remember me.

But I do know
late last night,
the dew hung on grass
just so
beautifully.

Now that counts for something,
doesn't it?

Prompt ~ Creative Genealogy ♥

Writing Exercise
Tools: Your *Leap Journal*, pen, and timer
Time: 20 minutes

Research is continually revealing new things about how we are all interconnected, and how our personal experiences can be impacted by people we don't even know, often in very subtle yet powerful ways. For example, we can be impacted by traumas experienced by previous generations, the beliefs of our families, communities, and cultures, or events on the other side of the world. Answer the following questions in your *Leap Journal*:

- How is achievement valued or perceived by your culture?
- How has achievement been valued and perceived by your family?
- How about creativity?
- How about intuition?
- What are some of the repeating stories you've heard about creativity or intuition?
- What were your ancestors' attitudes towards achievement, creativity and intuition? If you don't know for sure, what would your guess be?
- Think of a challenge you are experiencing in some area of your life. In what way are ideas that are not your own impacting your experience of this situation?

Prompt ~ Be Here Now ☀

Mindfulness Activity
Tools: Yourself!
Time: 3 minutes

Set a timer for three minutes and practice just being. Try to appreciate the small details of your surroundings and this moment, just as it is.

- Become aware of all your senses.
- Notice smells.
- Pay attention to sounds.
- Tune into sounds you usually block out.
- Pay attention to color and light.

Now repeat the exercise, tuning into yourself.

- How does the energy around your body feel?
- How about in your body?
- How are you feeling emotionally?
- Is there anything calling out for your attention?

> "*The miracle is to walk on the green earth in the present moment, to appreciate the peace and beauty that are available now.*"
>
> ~ *Thich Nhat Hanh*

Who's to Say?

Who's to say
that something's good?

If it's right,
punctuation perfect
words, phrases, just so?

Does it move you?

This is all I want to know.

Does it move you
from one place
to the next,
from one
emotional state
to another?

Sad to happy.

Slow to fast.

Even if you are angered
because this poem
is so bad

That pleases me.

Because it worked!

You knew the words
were on a journey

And you came too.

Prompt ~ The Art of Feeling ♥

Meditation + Writing Exercise
Tools: Your *Leap Journal* and a pen
Time: 10 minutes

Sometimes life can feel as if it is happening *to* us. It can be very empowering to realize that we have far more control over our experiences than we may realize.

Think of a time when your emotions took a major shift, like a mood swing. It might be a time when you were feeling happy, at the top of your game and someone said something that shattered your confidence or made you angry, or when you were feeling sad, and something happened that made you smile again.

Imagine you are seeing this experience from above, as if you are in the balcony of a theater and are looking down at yourself in this past event the way one would watch an actor in a play. From this perspective, what do you notice?

- What triggered you, causing your mood to change?
- What was the first thing you did when this happened?
- What did you think? How did you reveal this, perhaps through your facial expressions or actions?
- How did you respond physically?
- What did you say or what other choices did you make in response to the shift in your feelings?
- What thoughts and beliefs may have led to your response?

- What future beliefs or decisions did you make as a result of what happened?

Do this exercise for both positive and negative mood shifts, no matter how minor the mood changes may have been. Sometimes the minor mood changes are the most revealing.

- What habits do you have regarding how you emotionally respond to outer events?

- What assumptions do you habitually make?

- What might help you change your emotional experiences for the better?

Write down any insights you have in your *Leap Journal*.

> *"Acquire the habit of checking in with yourself. Several times a day, just take a beat, and ask yourself how you are feeling."*
>
> *~Julia Cameron*

Life as Art

When will we stop
looking at writers and artists and musicians
as different?

Do we really need genius
to know
how important it is
to pile blocks,
tend a garden,
mix colors,
create meaning
in this life?

Every motion
we each take matters,
even for those of us
who don't know the color wheel.

No, especially those of us
who do not know.

Those of us
who stumble
in the darkness
believing Creator's magic
belongs to someone else
have skipped the greatest truth,
the most important one

So basic,
we almost miss it.

That is:
Life Is Art.

Each moment
a brush stroke,
our heart playing out its colors
against the great big
Canvas
of the story of our lives.

Prompt ~ Art Exhibit ♥

Art Project
Tools: Your *Leap Journal*, pen, and colored pencils, paints, or crayons
Time: 10 minutes

Imagine you have been put in charge of creating multiple pieces of art, or large paintings, each one representing a different aspect of your life. Pretend that these works of art will be on display in an exhibit about you.

Map out a plan for these pieces of art in your *Leap Journal*.

- Come up with a list of topics for each piece of work such as love, home, career, hobbies, family, friends, etc.

- What would each piece of art look like?

- What would its vibe be?

- What colors would each include?

- Would there be any words or images?

- What conclusions might people make about you and your life by looking at each piece of art?

- What would you name each piece of art?

- What would you want this art exhibit to be called?

> *"What would it be like if you lived each day, each breath, as a work of art in progress?"*
>
> ~*Thomas Crum*

Just A Scribe

Will you stop?
I ask her.

When will you stop
delivering me poems?

Oh never,
she laughs,
then keeps weaving
as if an old woman
on a machine.

For now that you've
started listening
we have more
to pour
down on you,
through the top
of your head,
down into
your pen.

And so,
I keep it moving
as quick as I can,
trying to keep up
and to honor
this daunting task
I have been given
as Scribe.

Prompt ~ Honor the Task ☀

Meditation
Tools: A quiet, private place
Time: Five minutes

Imagine you have been given a task, a gift, a message to pass on that has flowed to you.

- Close your eyes and imagine this is happening right how, like a beautiful glowing light of goodness, flowing into you from above.

- Imagine receiving a word, message, sensation, feeling, idea, project, or talent you feel an urge or desire to share with others in some creative way.

Trust what comes. Write it down.

> *"Now is the time to know that all that you do is sacred."*
>
> *~Hafiz*

Sometimes I Panic

Sometimes I panic.

I don't want to die
before I deliver this poem.

Handing it off to someone else
feels that important.

Prompt ~ Accepting Purpose ☑

Writing Exercise
Tools: Your *Leap Journal*, pen, and timer
Time: 20 minutes

Have you ever felt a burning desire to accomplish something before you die? Have you ever had a thought that if you didn't complete something specific before your death you would regret it?

How about things you would want people to know, gifts, or legacies you want to pass on to loved ones?

- Make a list.
- Prioritize your list in order of tasks or legacies based on how important they feel right now at this point in your life.
- Circle one that is calling to you the loudest.

Make a plan. Take the first step. Tell someone.

> *"Don't give up trying to do what you really want to do. Where there is love and inspiration, I don't think you can go wrong."*
>
> *~Ella Fitzgerald*

Day Off

Take a day off from writing?
I can't imagine.

Because the factory
will still be running.

Who will be there
to collect the goods?

Prompt ~ Playtime ☑

Writing Exercise
Tools: Your *Leap Journal* and a pen
Time: 10 minutes

Write your answers to the following questions in your *Leap Journal*:

- What are those things that you could do all day, no matter what?
- What are those things that to you feel like play even if to others they might feel like work?
- What are those things that come easily to you?
- What are those tasks other people often ask you to do, or about which they come to you for advice?
- What activities bring you the most joy?

> *"I am in the world only for the purpose of composing."*
>
> ~*Franz Schubert*

Finding Words

I sit
and
watch
and
wonder.

What is this life of mine about?

Why do I
search
and
grasp
for the
perfect word
for each remaining space?

Why does it matter so much?

I only know that
it does.

Prompt ~ Your Secret Mission ☀

Life Practice
Tools: Daily life, your *Leap Journal*, and a pen
Time: One week

One of the keys to connecting with our callings is knowing what motivates and drives us. The clearer we are about the reasons behind our actions—those aligned with our True Selves and those driven by other unmet emotional needs—the easier it becomes to make slight adjustments so that our lives become more fully aligned with our most positive Selves.

What if you were on a secret mission to boost the positive energy of the world? How might this "Secret Mission" game change the way you approach how you live your life or do your work?

- This week, pretend you are on a secret mission to make the world a brighter place and see what happens. Have fun with this. Imagine you are a kid playing make-believe.

- Notice what old, habitual patterns fall away when uplifting yourself and others becomes your primary focus.

What new behaviors do you adopt, or choices do you make as a result? Do you feel a greater sense of purpose or passion for life?

> *"When you know who you are; when your mission is clear and you burn with the inner fire of unbreakable will; no cold can touch your heart; no deluge can dampen your purpose. You know that you are alive."*
>
> ~*Chief Seattle*

Unpacking a Story

Unpacking a story
Like a suitcase

We discover
hidden treasures
and old, dirty socks.

Which one are we?

Prompt ~ Unpacking Me ♥

Writing Exercise
Tools: Your *Leap Journal* and a pen
Time: 20 minutes

Knowing ourselves is power. Imagine your life is packed up in a suitcase—your past, present, and future are all safely inside. Pretend a stranger finds it and opens it up.

Write down your answers to the following in your *Leap Journal*:

- What would they discover?
- What might they learn about you, your hopes and dreams, intuitive nudges, and relationship with your creative voice?
- What assumptions (whether right or wrong) might they make?
- What might surprise them?

Complete the following sentences:

- Something that embarrasses me about my life is…
- A secret technique I use to get more done is…
- A secret trick that works for me is…
- Something I love about how I live my life is…
- A secret creative dream I have is…

> *"I've come to believe that we all carry clear, precise maps of our futures inside us."*
>
> ~*Martha Beck*

Polaris

I reached up to the sky
and pulled down something wonderful.

Even now,
it guides me still.

Prompt ~ What's Calling You? ☀

Writing Exercise
Tools: Your *Leap Journal* and a pen
Time: 10 minutes

Take a deep breath, close your eyes. After a few minutes of turning inward, open your eyes and complete the following sentences in your *Leap Journal*:

- In the privacy of my own heart, I hear…
- I am feeling called by…
- This is calling my name…

Prompt ~ How Are You Growing? ☀

Writing Exercise
Tools: Your *Leap Journal* and a pen
Time: 10 minutes

Answer the following questions in your *Leap Journal*:

- What's an area of your life that feels small, where you are ready to expand?
- What's something you haven't admitted to anyone else, maybe not even to yourself?
- How are you ready to grow?

> *"If the only thing you ever did was fill your life with the people, things, and activities that bring you genuine joy, you'd find your North Star almost immediately."*
>
> *~Martha Beck*

What Soothes You?

What is your thing?

The thing that fills you up
when your soul grows parched and dry?

What brings you comfort?

Is it strawberries?
A sunset?
A long sip of an ice-cold beverage
or warm tea with honey and lemon?

Or is it a paintbrush
dipped in acrylics or oils
brushed across a canvas for only you to see?

Is it a butterfly
landing softly on a flower
drinking sweet nectar
then flying off
as if it never was?

What warms you when you are cold?

Perhaps a campfire
as you cuddle with a loved one,
close enough to see one spark
giving birth to more,
exploding upward,
grey smoke rising,
a pop so close and loud
you feel like you've escaped gunshot,
dramatically thawed from the inside out,
scorching hot
but not close enough to burn?

Or is it hot sand
on your cold feet
or sizzling skin on the entire back of your body
as you flop onto the baking beach
after a springtime swim
in icy ocean water?

What quenches your thirst?

Is it a fizzy drink
bubbling in a clear glass jar
as you watch the bubbles rise
circular, curling,
rising to the top
where they cluster
then divide
as your straw
enters their field
breaking them apart
and you feel those bubbles in you
all the way down to your toes?

What fills you up?

After you've taken cardboard box after box
out to the curb
or to the dump
or to the goodwill collection box
then turned back to hear your own echo
against empty walls and hard floors,
ripped off carpets
emptied of memories as you prepare to
begin again?

What warms your heart?

On those mornings
when a full day lies before you
no plans
no guests
no distractions
from the inner voice that has waited
so long
to be heard?

What clears your mind?

When you think you are alone
and are not sure what you're feeling, exactly.
Is it loneliness?
Sadness?
Emptiness?
Or quiet excitement
building at the prospect of nothing left to do?

What fuels your Inner Creator?

Emptiness?
Questions?
Encouragement?
Nature?
Sounds of beating waves
against the sand
like a shaman's drum?

What is your name?

When there is no one left to
remember who you were,
when your own babyhood has gotten
washed away
as if by a flood
tearing down the gutters
rushing down the street
picking up speed
faster and faster
past houses and driveways
luring children
to rinse their ankles
splashing in puddles as it passes
before rain merges with overflowing
streams and dreams
heading to the sewer grates and
out to the bay
and then the sun comes out again
so hot and parched and searing
that no one remembers.

What soothes your soul?

Is it a cool rag dipped in ice water
and rose petals
resting across eyelids with a
gentle touch,
a healing whisper,
a wish
for all that is in
your highest good?

Or an empty page
in a new journal
or blank sketchbook,
freshly sharpened pencils,
pastels, crayons, charcoal,
a soft spot to sit upon in the woods,
thick bark of a redwood friend
to lean up against
so you can rest and sketch,
no one noticing you've gone missing
until the sunset
stretches across the sky
and the sun sinks down, saying
adieu to another empty, open day?

What soothes you, then?

Prompt ~ What Soothes You? ☑

Writing Exercise
Tools: Your *Leap Journal* and a pen
Time: 10 minutes

Our passions are the key to who we really are and the unique gifts we have to offer the world. They can also be a huge source of comfort when times are tough. Answer the below questions from this poem in your *Leap Journal*.

- What is your *thing*?
- What brings you comfort?
- What warms you when you are cold?
- What quenches your thirst?
- What fills you up?
- What warms your heart?
- What clears your mind?
- What fuels your Inner Creator?
- What would your name be if there were no one left to remember?
- What soothes your soul?

> *"Occasionally, in life there are those moments of unutterable fulfillment which cannot be completely explained by those symbols called words. Their meanings can only be articulated by the inaudible language of the heart."*
>
> *~Martin Luther King, Jr.*

Beginnings

How will I know
if I'm finished?

Finished?

Oh no.

You never will be,
says a voice
from some other place.

I look around,
wanting to continue the conversation.

But she is gone.

Ending must be a little bit like dying.

At some point, we have to take
a final breath,
knowing we are done here.

But we are never really done.

Like a string,
drawing us out of ourselves
from this time,
this life,
this chapter,
pulling us
at times,
relentlessly

at times,
against our will

at times,
with gentle invitation
to what's next

Inviting us
to close
so we can open,
to come
so we can go

Inviting us
to get on with it,
the inevitable dive
from the very edge
of the board
into what's next.

Every ending
then,
a beginning.

Prompt ~ Beginning and Completing ♥

Writing Exercise
Tools: Your *Leap Journal* and a pen
Time: 10 minutes

Answer the following questions in your *Leap Journal:*

- What's coming to an end in your life?
- What's something you really want to complete?
- What's something you are ready to begin?
- What's your next inevitable creative dive from the edge of the board?

"Whatever you do, or dream you can, begin it. Boldness has genius and power and magic in it."

~Johann Wolfgang von Goethe

Self-Reflection

~Honoring Your Callings~

When we talk about callings or our purpose, we often come up against the idea that our callings are something we were born to do, and if we deviate, we will somehow have failed. What if, instead, our callings are simply the moment-by-moment guidance we are all receiving all the time about how to let our True Selves shine?

Write your answers to the following questions in your *Leap Journal*:

- If you had one week to do anything you wanted, how would you spend your time?
- What's an activity that makes you lose track of time?
- What do you think your favorite friend or closest loved ones would say about who you really are?
- What do you think your younger self would say about what really makes you happy and what you love to do?
- Imagine yourself as 20 years older than you are now. What do you think your older self would say is the most important gift you are giving to others (even without you realizing it)?
- What do you know, beyond a shadow of a doubt, to be true?
- What is a simple message you would like to share with the world?

- What is one dream you hope to see come true before you die?
- What's one small thing you can do to help that dream happen?

What's Your Leap?

What's something you would love to do but aren't sure you're good at? How can you do that more often?

Your Next Leap

Where are you headed?

When I was young, on hot, humid, summer days in New Jersey, our family used to go a local swimming pool near our home. At the deep end, there were two diving boards. One was about three feet off the ground. The other was more than 10 feet high.

I'll never forget the first time I climbed the ladder leading up to that high dive, grasping the cold metal rungs, one after the next as the other kids watched my every move, eager for their turns. When I reached the top, I couldn't believe how far the pool looked beneath me. My stomach clenched and flip-flopped. The gritty rough surface of the board scraped my feet and every single muscle in my body contracted as I slowly inched my way down the board, which wobbled beneath me. Far below, the other kids stared up at me, making noises of impatience as they jockeyed for their places in line.

Would they laugh at me if I asked them to wait a little bit longer and get out of the way as I climbed back down again? Was that even possible? Or, if I turned around on the narrow platform now quivering, would I slip off the side and fall?

I felt an overwhelming sense of anxiety and regret. If I wasn't already so embarrassed by how slowly I was moving, I probably would have gotten down on my hands and knees, and clamored back down that ladder instead of taking the leap into the cold, deep water far below.

I'm pretty sure I've blocked out that moment when I finally let go and leaped. What I do remember, however, is the liberation I felt seconds after my feet left the board and I was hanging mid-air. Time slowed down and I felt invincible, as if I could do anything.

That summer, my climbs up that tall ladder became easier and easier, yet those mid-air moments always retained their magic. By the end of the summer, I had joined the other kids in using those moments in mid-air to contort my body into spins, somersaults, making silly faces, feigning salutes, and pretending to be animals or characters made up on the spot. No longer were the eyes on me filled with impatience and judgement. Instead, they reflected my own excitement. We were bonded through our shared understanding of the joy of the leap.

It's easy to get lulled into thinking that courage is revealed in those moments when we are mid-air and the whole world can see what we've just done. Real courage, instead, is what happens during those private inner leaps we take with an audience of one. Before we direct our outer actions toward where our creative energy wants us to go, we first must confer with our inner voice, that peaceful Self within. When we have the courage to have honest, vulnerable, authentic, loving, encouraging conversations with ourselves like a best friend would—that's when real transformation happens.

The call to leap is like a whisper awakening us from a deep sleep. We open our eyes, thinking we've been imagining things. As we go through the motions of our lives, we have the sense that something is trying to get our attention. It may feel like something is beckoning to us to expand us beyond the limits of our current lives. Ultimately, the calling to leap is a thirst for ourselves.

Our strength is revealed in those quiet moments when we know it's time to do something different and we admit it to ourselves for the very first time. Acceptance comes first, before we make the choice to do something about what is calling to us. Acceptance is a private act;

it happens not in community but rather alone, in the quietness of our own hearts.

Acceptance is like a conversation between us and our God. Acceptance is a confession, an opening, a switch turned on. After we accept, the call for a leap happens. We commit and the cycle begins.

Leaping requires muscle—a minute movement of muscles, one after the next, firing in sequence, a contraction and crouching down. We need something to push off against and so, we lean in. When we get to the core, the heart of who we are, we find the courage to leap.

Before we rise, we first double down. We connect with the earth, the ground, our integrity, our roots, our foundation, our platform, making sure our springboard is in good form. Before sharing our unique gifts in a way that can help others, we first must accept and claim them for ourselves. Contracting muscles turn inward. We shrink to expand, folding first into ourselves so that when we spring upward, we rise as high as we can possibly go.

Only you know what next little act of courage is in your highest good, or what's going to help you to keep moving in the direction that is right for *you*. My wish is that when you leap, you experience the joy, freedom, and possibilities that so often happen when we are mid-air, and *anything* can happen. May you also connect with your own compassion, courage, and confidence, as well as a feeling of being energetically supported by intuitive, creative friends as you find your wings and follow where *your* true, creative voice is guiding *you* to go.

> *"No single energy can be more impactful on this planet than the joy and well-being emanating from one truly happy and loving person."*
>
> *~Barry Kaufman*

When We Decide

When we decide
we don't need to
sound smart
or even wise,
that we don't care
about leaving our mark
or even footprints behind,
when we let go of all that,
only then
will we start to hear
what our heart
really wants to say.

Prompt ~ Invitation from Your Heart ☀

Meditation
Tools: Your *Leap Journal* and a pen
Time: 10 minutes

Imagine you just received an invitation from your heart. You open the envelope slowly, and as you pull out what's inside, you realize that your heart is inviting you to start something new and exciting, to take a leap.

Close your eyes and imagine this is happening now.

- What project or exciting new thing is your heart inviting you to start?

Have fun with this. Let yourself be surprised. The project doesn't have to be realistic, achievable, or even anything you've considered before. It doesn't have to make sense.

There is no hierarchy when it comes to dreams of the heart. If it's calling to you from within, it matters. Trust what comes to you. Pay attention and see what your imagination and creative voice have to say.

We often don't know where one fleeting idea will take us next. It's impossible to see the full picture of our lives. All we can do is follow each creative, wonderful idea and see where it takes us next. Sometimes, we get so attached to a certain vision of how our lives are supposed to be that we don't even consider options that might, for us, be even better.

Prompt ~ A Color, Symbol, and Sound ☀

Meditation + Writing Exercise
Tools: Your *Leap Journal* and a pen
Time: 10 minutes

If you had to choose a color, symbol, sound, or song to represent the invitation you received in the *Invitation from the Heart* meditation on the previous page, what might these be?

Close your eyes and focus on your breath. Trust whatever comes to you from a deeply relaxed state. Often the first thing that pops into our minds is the most important.

Write it down in your *Leap Journal*.

Prompt ~ As If It's Already Happened ☀

Writing Exercise
Tools: Your *Leap Journal* and a pen
Time: 10 minutes

What might your life be like after you've said YES to your heart's invitation?

Complete the following sentences:

- This could happen...
- So could this...
- I would love it if this would happen...
- Maybe this could even happen...
- Something that would be unexpected but wonderful would be if...

Write about all positive possibilities in your *Leap Journal*. Describe your best possible scenario, down to the detail.

Prompt ~ When You Decide ☑

Writing Exercise
Tools: Your *Leap Journal* and a pen
Time: 10 minutes

The minute we decide we are ready for our lives to change, and we are willing to do what it takes to support those changes, life really starts to pick up speed.

Answer the following questions in your *Leap Journal*:

- What's something you really want to change in your life?
- What's something your soul really wants you to create?
- What's something you would do if you didn't care what anyone thought?
- What's your next creative leap?

Prompt ~ What's Your First Step? ☑

Writing Exercise + Life Practice
Tools: Your *Leap Journal*, pen, and any tools needed to take the first step toward your heart's invitation
Time: One week

Write a list in your *Leap Journal* of all the tasks that you need to do to fulfill the *Invitation From Your Heart* prompt, or any wish calling to you from within.

After you've completed your list, go back and next to each item, estimate how much time you think each task will take to do.

Look at your calendar for this week. When can you do the first step on your list? Block out the time. Be relaxed about this. Resist the temptation to become rigid or to set too high expectations, or to look too far ahead. View your first to-do simply as a starting point, a rung on the ladder to your metaphoric high dive.

Once you have completed the first step, congratulate yourself. Celebrate. Tell someone. Do a happy dance. Check it off!

Then, go back to your list, and schedule the next task on your list. Do something special for yourself each time you complete one of the steps on your list. Keep doing this and feel your energy and your life pick up momentum.

Prompt ~ Creating Your *Leaped List* ☑

Writing Exercise
Tools: Your *Leap Journal* and a pen
Time: 10 minutes

Honoring how far we've come is very helpful in keeping our energy high and moving forward.

- Create a list of leaps you've taken in your life. These can include any choices or decisions you made that were truly aligned with who you really are, or where your true inner voice was calling you to go. How it all turned out, or whether your leaps were graceful or perfectly executed doesn't matter. Any leap we take on our own behalf is significant. Write them all down. This is your *Leaped List.*

Examples of leaps might be making a new friend, restarting a beloved hobby, or making a request we are not sure will be answered. It also can be something small, like pausing, taking a deep breath, or taking the first step towards releasing a habit that is no longer good for us.

- Make this list an active, constantly growing list. Anytime you do something that affirms your value or honors a whisper from that soft still voice within, add it to your *Leaped List.*

Self-affirming leaps are how we trigger a chain reaction of synchronicities that can lead to miracles.

- Bookmark your *Leaped List* in your *Leap Journal.*

- Make sure you leave plenty of blank space at the end.

- Add to this list on an ongoing basis.

Prompt ~ Creating Your *To-Leap List* ☑

Writing Exercise
Tools: Your *Leap Journal* and a pen
Time: 10 minutes

In addition to keeping track of leaps we complete, it can also be helpful to make a list of leaps we want to take in the future.

This is not your regular to-do list. It's a place to dream, brainstorm, and challenge yourself to let your light shine! Include actions that will fill with you joy or you know for sure are in your best interest, even if they require courage.

The idea is to create a list of simple action steps that will move your life in a direction that is aligned with the unique energy of your True Self. There is incredible power in actions that do this. When we live in alignment with who we are, we often attract unexpected new opportunities that can change our lives.

Check off items on your *To-Leap List* when you have completed them. Leave space at the end to add new leaps you want to take. Keep brainstorming and checking things off!

When you accomplish items on this *To-Leap List*, remember to add them to your *Leaped List* (from the prompt on the previous page) and celebrate all that you've accomplished on your own behalf.

Prompt ~ Who's In Your Corner? ☑

Writing Exercise
Tools: Your *Leap Journal* and a pen
Time: 10 minutes

Make a list of all the people you can count on to support you as you prepare to take leaps—not for permission or approval, but those who truly believe in you, have confidence in your abilities to connect with and follow your True Self, and who truly want what is best for you.

- Consider having regular check-in meetings with friends who you know will support you.
- How can you support them too?
- Talk with a friend and decide how you can support each other in a way that works well for both of you.
- Write down your commitments.

Prompt ~ Strengthen Your Springboard ☑

Writing Exercise
Tools: Your *Leap Journal* and a pen
Time: 10 minutes

Make a list in your *Leap Journal* of all the ways you can support yourself in taking more leaps.

Ideas might include taking a course, joining a group, going to the library, doing online research, buying supplies, setting aside time, creating space, getting therapy, saying no, setting boundaries, making a commitment, or any other action steps that became clear as you completed the prompts in this book.

See *Section Four* of this book for additional sources of support.

> *"All we have to decide is what to do with the time that is given us."*
>
> *~J.R.R. Tolkien*

You Don't Need Permission

I don't need permission.

I don't need the permission
of a teacher, coach, or parent.
I don't need permission
from society, a group, committee, or government.
I don't need permission
from a child, friend, partner or neighbor.
I don't need permission
from a church, minister, priest, or the world.

I don't need permission.

I don't even have to make them understand first
Even if they desperately want me to explain
Even they think I should help them
before I follow my calling.

I don't need permission from anyone or anything –
be it a university, school, diploma,
or even my own past deeds or declarations.

I don't need permission

To be great
To be strong
To be intuitive
To be confident
To be a leader
To be trustworthy
To be whole.

All I need is to do whatever my Soul
tells me is right
for me in this moment.

I am not a victim.
I am not a child.
I am not trapped.
I am not a prisoner.
I am not bad or wrong.

My choices are not wrong either,
especially when I am following my truth.

I don't need permission.

To value, care for, and protect my own Self,
to choose to honor my deepest knowing and
follow my own heart.

I don't need permission
to do what my Soul is calling me to do
without apology, anger, or explanation,
without telling my story or
living up to anyone's else's expectations.

I don't need permission

To be inspirational
To be successful
To be powerful

And in charge of my own life.

I don't need permission

To be happy
To shine
To laugh
To love
To dance to my own beat
or to say what in my heart I know to be true.

I don't need permission
to do what I think is best.

I don't need anyone else's permission
to be the truest, most beautiful,
amazing, powerful, gifted me.

And neither do You.

Prompt ~ Give Yourself Permission 

Writing Exercise
Tools: Your *Leap Journal* and a pen
Time: 10 minutes

I wrote *You Don't Need Permission* more than a decade before the other poems in this book. I was doing the dishes, and found my mind wandering off, imagining a fictious conversation with a previous writing teacher. At the time, I had a blog and realized that I was indirectly looking for reassurance or permission from some outer source to do what my true voice was calling me to do.

In my work and conversations with friends, I have found that this habit of looking outward for a seal of approval or a sign that we are meant to do what is calling to us from our true, inner voice is very common. Most of us have a part of our personality that doesn't fully trust the True Self. Many of us have been socialized to question our own inner wisdom, or to put others' authority above our own.

I don't know if you ever find yourself looking for outer confirmation or reassurance before trusting your own inner wisdom, but if so, this prompt can help.

Think of an area of your life, or perhaps some aspect of the dream you identified in the *Invitation from your Heart* prompt about which you might be waiting for some outer sign, guidance, or perhaps reassurance from some outer source before moving forward.

How could you be there for yourself the way you might wish an expert, mentor, parent, partner, or all-mighty being would be? What might change if you were to really give yourself permission to trust what you know and want, and to honor it through *action*?

When we put things in writing, they often have more power than when we simply think the thoughts or speak the words.

In your *Leap Journal*, write down a promise to yourself about something that matters to you deeply.

You might begin:

- I hereby give myself permission to...
- I am as worthy as anyone else in manifesting this dream because...
- I promise to support myself in taking leaps in the following ways...
- Here's how I promise to protect my hopes and dreams...
- I promise to demonstrate my full approval of myself by...
- I promise to show my trust and confidence in my True Self by taking these actions...

> *"One has just to be oneself. That's my basic message. The moment you accept yourself as you are, all burdens, all mountainous burdens simply disappear. Then life is a sheer joy, a festival of lights."*
>
> *~Bhagwan Shree Rajneesh*

Silently Together

Intake and outtake.

In breath
and
out breath.

Drawing in.
Letting go.

Life is like this,
I think.

When we forget
to do one
without the other

It's like a marriage
ill-matched.

Dance step
gone wrong.

Toes squashed.

Lovers apart
who would much rather be
side by side
rowing in the same boat.

Separate but equal.

In synch with Self and Soul,
with every wave
and each other.

Silently together.

Breathe in.

Breathe out.

This is how,
I think,
everything works.

Prompt ~ Keep Shining Bright ☑

Writing Exercise
Tools: Your *Leap Journal* and a pen
Time: 10 minutes

Life has a natural creative rhythm. There are times when we need to pause, rest, retreat, and reconnect with that soft still voice within. Other times, we may feel completely clear, energized, filled with passion, and ready to move forward. The more we come to know, trust, and respect our natural rhythm, the clearer we become about when it's time to fill up and restore our energy and when it's time to leap.

A dream is like a marathon with lots of little leaps along the way. What do you need to do to keep yourself strong for the journey ahead?

What's something you can do to keep your energy high as you start to take more creative leaps in your life? Ideas might include doing little things each day that bring you joy. Pay attention to sleep, diet, fresh air, and exercise.

Write it all down in your *Leap Journal.*

Prompt ~ Breathing Through Your Next Leap ☀

Meditation and Mindfulness
Tools: You
Time: Three minutes

Everything in life runs according to this undulating schedule of in-breath and out-breath, rise and fall, night and day, peak and valley, up and down. For this prompt, we are going to simply use our breath to remind ourselves how supported we are.

Sometimes just being aware of what we need and where we are at in our own inner rhythm of input and output can make all the difference. This is a brief meditative exercise we can do as we go throughout the motions of living busy lives.

With each inhale, we can imagine attracting to us everything that we most need. With every exhale, we can imagine letting go of everything that we no longer need. The more we do this exercise of letting go and welcoming support, the more balanced we often start to feel, and the easier leaping becomes.

- Breathe in and imagine welcoming in all that is in your best interest.

- Breathe out and imagine releasing everything that you no longer need to be the best version of yourself, and to live your best life.

We are each part of nature, an integral part of the inhaling and exhaling that is happening all around us. By embracing both our core humanity and our True Nature, we make leaping a way of life.

> *"Go confidently in the direction of your dreams! Live the life you've imagined. As you simplify your life, the laws of the universe will be simpler."*
>
> *~Henry David Thoreau*

Self-Reflection

~Taking Your Next Leap~

The more conversations we have with our soft, still voice within, the easier leaping becomes. Each tiny creative and intuitive leap is like a magic key. When we turn it, the next leap we need to take becomes revealed.

Here are a few questions to help you to hear the next little leaps your True Self is ready to take. Write your answers in your *Leap Journal*:

- What's a change you are ready to create?
- What's something you feel led to do that requires letting go of what others think of you?
- Open this book to another page. How does the message on that page apply to your life right now?
- Open this book to any page. Pay attention to the first word that jumps out at you. How might that word relate to an important next step in some area of your life?
- Choose a poem from this book that resonates with you. Which words or phrases ring true to you? How could this be guidance for you and your life?
- What's a small leap you can take right now to let your True Self know you've heard its call?

What's Your Leap?

What's a leap you are ready to take?

"Leap, and the net will appear."

~Julia Cameron

Strengthening Your Springboard

Leap Reminders

As we end our journey together, I want to share a few final tips and reminders that have helped me. If you ever have a day when your life isn't flowing or you feel creatively stuck (we all have them!), these may help.

You Are Not Alone

There is a whole community of others who, at some point or another, have experienced the same emotions you might be feeling right now, whether stuck, apprehensive, enthusiastic, or energized. If you find yourself faltering, lean into your safe people. Lean also into your True Self and keep expanding your circle.

Invite others to join you in activities that are meaningful to you. Practice being vulnerable. Get curious about people who are different than yourself. Be on the lookout for ideas, gifts, and opportunities that may come from unexpected places.

Also remember, it's okay to be imperfect. We are all human and are always doing the best we can. Strive to spend time with people whose energy makes you feel healthy and strong, and with whom you can really be yourself. Strive to be that type of person for others.

When all else fails, keep doing your joyful daily activities. Keep moving, listening, and creating. Your positive energy, creative flow, and synchronicities will attract others to you just when you need them most.

Follow Your Joy

We are often looking for the "thing"—that piece of wisdom, or the professional or friend who is going to help us when we feel stuck. It's important to seek help and support when we need it. It's also important to remember that we are each responsible for keeping ourselves inspired and connected to our True Selves.

Every day, as much as is possible, find inspiration. Seek joy. This can be as simple as looking out the window and noticing how beautiful the day is or appreciating a stranger's smile. It doesn't take much to find something that can shift our perspective. The key is making up our mind that staying inspired is the most important thing we do in each day.

Trust What Works for YOU

When you find something that brings you joy and gets your creativity and life flowing, hold onto it. We can overthink our creative processes as if they are mysteries we need to figure out with charts, graphs, and time management formulas. Sometimes, however, getting life to flow is as simple as giving ourselves permission to do what brings us joy and feels right, to trust what we know works for us.

Find Your Tribe (and Stay Open)

For a long time, I didn't think I needed a creative community. After all, writing is really a private act. In fact, I found that too much socializing, or being too busy in the outer world kept me from making my art or staying attuned to my own personal formula for being creative and feeling inner peace.

I have since learned that having a creative circle isn't about appointments, new obligations, socializing, or commitments. Instead, it's about being part of a larger ebb and flow that supports our own inner highs and lows. Being part of a larger, invisible creative circle is about give and take, like the necessary in-breath and out-breath that keeps us alive. In a supportive, healthy creative community, we are both of service and open to receiving what we need when we most need it.

It can be amazing how simply shifting our intention and our perspective can draw inspiring, creative, intuitive people to us. Life is filled with serendipities and beginnings that look like endings. Affirm you want a supportive creative tribe, and you will likely find one. It makes all the difference when we are ready, well-poised to say yes, to welcome the gifts others offer us with gratitude and humility, and to give, give, give, as well as to receive.

Say YES to Your Calling

We get so many mixed messages about what it means to do our work in the world. These outside messages can get in the way of us honoring what is uniquely right for us. When we practice looking at ourselves through the eyes of a loving being who truly loves us deeply and unconditionally, something usually shifts. When we can imagine being completely loved and accepted exactly as we are with no need to change to deserve this love, and even more importantly, no power to change this love by our own imperfections, slowly we start to love ourselves and others in that way too.

Our love muscle is revealed in the creative work we produce and the way we live our lives. I believe that feeling intuitively called to do something in the world means we will be supported. It also means trusting that each person in the world has something important and of value to offer, and that includes us. The more we trust that we have gifts to offer, and the more we lean into a creative energy that is bigger than each of us individually, the more supported we tend to feel.

You are a gift to this world simply because you exist. You bless the earth with each breath you take. Your energy shines in ways you don't even know. When we settle into the knowing that no matter what happens in the outer world, we are lovable and a miracle, and that far more is happening than meets the eye, life starts to flow in wonderful new directions.

You are the answer to an invitation and a question from the universe; your heart's invitation echoes that greater invitation that has already been fulfilled by you being here. Your callings are simply an extension of the miraculous energy of who you really are. The more joyful leaps we each take, the more expansive the world becomes.

> *"We do not need magic to change the world, we carry all the power we need inside ourselves already."*
>
> ~ *J.K. Rowling*

The Art of Leaping

Leaping is about movement. It's not just about moving forward; it's about actively choosing to have a new experience.

When we take creative leaps, we rise up and almost always end up somewhere new.

When we leap, we invite and welcome in the unknown.

Leaping is always about change. That's because when we leap, we do something different than we were the moment before.

Leaps don't last forever.

Leaps always require pausing and getting grounded before we take the next one.

A leap never starts mid-air; we need a strong foundation to push off against to rise.

Taking a leap almost always requires some level of courage, self-knowledge, and acceptance.

Leaps are almost always fun. Rarely do we see people leaping upward without some sense of levity and joy.

Leaps are about progress, not perfection. They are often messy. They also often make us look and feel silly. As soon as we accept that the very nature of leaping is messy, leaping starts to become more fun.

Leaping requires the decision to do so. We can be pushed or pulled; leaping, however, is a choice.

Leaping is always a departure; we leave the familiar for the unpredictable.

Leaping requires risk. We rarely know where we are going to land, or what the outer conditions will be when we do. Often, however, not leaping has its risks too.

Leaping requires muscles, focus, and strength—figuratively, mentally, and physically.

Leaping leads to freedom—there is always a moment in mid-air when anything can happen.

Leaping can be a lot more fun when others are leaping along with us.

Whenever we take a creative leap, the energy around us leaps too.

Every creative act is a leap.

"It's like the man who comes to the tree at the fork in the road and says, 'Which way shall I go, this way or that?'

Go! Take one way and go!"

~Guru Rhh

The Language of Leaping: Glossary

Here is a quick glossary of some of the terms I used throughout this book, and what these words mean to me when it comes to finding and following our true, creative voice.

Leap ~ A leap is any action we take that is in alignment with our True Selves. Leaps often take us out of our comfort zone and feel like they take our life higher or align us with some higher purpose. When we leap, the energy of our True Self shines.

The True Self ~ The True Self is based on the idea that we each have a unique essence, a peaceful energy within that knows what is in our best interest. In psychology, this essence is sometimes called the egoless self, essential self, authentic self, intuition, or inner witness. Some spiritual practices refer to this energy as our Inner Light, unconditional love, God within, Buddha nature, soul, presence, or creative Muse. Yogic traditions refer to an innate goodness, softness, or a tenderness in our hearts we might sense during meditation. While we may have different ideas about what the True Self is, there is a general agreement across traditions that a peaceful energy and essence of open potential exists within each of us. Throughout this book, I refer to all these things as the True Self.

Intuition ~ This book is rooted in the idea that there is a soft, still voice constantly guiding us regarding what is in our highest good. I call this our intuition, creative voice, or the voice of the True Self. We all have other inner voices too, like our Inner Critics. This book is about turning up the volume on the True Self's loving voice and restoring it as our primary rudder, guiding us through life like an Ideal Parent.

Flow ~ Throughout the book I use flow to mean two different things:

- ***Flow state*** is the psychological state or zone where we lose track of time, our performance peaks, and creative ideas come to us more easily. Examples might include a runner's high, the hyperfocus an artist, musician, or athlete might experience while practicing their craft, or the soft awareness or presence a young child feels while playing a game. During a flow state, we often become fully immersed in what we are doing and lose track of what others are thinking of us. We also often feel more connected to others and the world, and after flow, have a stronger sense of confidence and awareness of who we really are.

- ***Life flow*** is a feeling of being supported by an outer energy that is greater than ourselves. Life flow is how it feels when we experience synchronicities aligned with our own intuition or highest good. It can feel as if our overall lives are flowing along in a positive way with little effort, or as if things are happening easily for us. Life flow often seems to increase the more we take leaps that honor who we really are.

Creativity (or Creative Flow) ~ Creativity is the flow of new ideas that peak when we are in a flow state. We are all creative. We each have different stories, experiences, perspectives, and a unique inner essence that contribute to our unique brand of creativity.

Gift ~ Our gift is the energy of our True Self. When this unique energy shines, we offer the world a gift that no one else can.

Finding What You Need: Menu of Prompts

Here's a quick guide to which prompts focus on common issues and struggles we all experience. My hope is that this quick guide will help you find prompts that can support you with what you need most on your own personal journey at this point in time.

Setting Boundaries

Healing Relationships

Integrating Your Past

Self-Awareness/Self-Acceptance

Finding Your Purpose/Passion

Connecting with Your True Self

Manifesting Your Dreams

Boosting Your Creativity/Intuition

Becoming More Present

Life Management

Complete Index to *The Seven Creative Touchstones* Essays, Poems, and Prompts

Touchstone 1: Inspiration

Section 3: Blocks

Section 4: Life

Section 5: Circles

Section 6: Callings

Section 7: Your Next Leap

References and Resources

Everything I have offered in this book is what I have learned through my own life journey, what I am continuing to learn through my own practices, my professional experiences, as well as an integration of wisdom from many different sources, teachers, and influences. I am deeply grateful to the authors, editors, artists, writers, poets, scholars, teachers, publications, programs, and creations cited here. While in no way all-inclusive, following are resources that have inspired me and influenced my outlook on life and my work—my own invisible circle of support.

The list includes teachers, many of whom I have studied with in person, as well as the resources from which I found the quotes included in this book. While I have done my best to provide credit to all copyrighted sources, I apologize for any omissions or errors. I take no responsibility for the accuracy or changing of information in cited sources, or the deletion of information from the Internet post-publication.

Thank you, each of you, alive and deceased, for taking your own creative leaps! My life's work, personal growth, and well-being have been enriched because of you sharing your voice, creativity, wisdom, and ideas. I am deeply grateful.

allgreatquotes.com

andiesantopietro.com

Ashiedu, B., *Inspirational Quotes for Women*, Insignia Expressions Limited, San Bernardino, CA, 2016.

Atripaldi, Gabriele, *365 Thoughts of Peace and Hope*, White Star Publishers, Novara, Italy, 2014.

azquotes.com

Barks, Coleman, *The Essential Rumi*, Castle Books, Edison, NJ, 1995.

Beattie, Melody, *The Language of Letting Go*, Harper Collins Publishers, New York, NY, 1990.

Beck, Martha, *Finding Your Own North Star: Claiming the Life We Were Meant to Live,* Harmony Books, New York, NY, 2002.

birdwatchingbuzz.com/hummingbird-symbolism

Brach, Tara, Ph.D., *Radical Acceptance: Embracing Your Life with The Heart of a Buddha,* Bantam Books, New York, 2003.

brainyquote.com

Brown, Brené, *Braving the Wilderness: The Quest for True Belonging and the Courage to Stand Alone,* Random House, New York, 2018.

Brown, Brené, *Dare To Lead: Brave Work. Tough Conversations. Whole Hearts,* Random House, New York, 2018.

Brown, Brené, *The Gifts of Imperfection: Let Go of Who You Think You're Supposed to Be and Embrace Who You Are*, Hazelden Publishing, New York, 2010.

Brown, Brené, brenebrown.com/articles/2018/05/24/the-midlife-unraveling

Caddy, Eileen, *Footprints on the Path,* Findhorn Press, Scotland, UK, 1991.

Caddy, Eileen, *Opening Doors Within,* Findhorn Press, Scotland, UK, 1986.

Cameron, Julia, *The Artist's Way: A Spiritual Path to Higher Creativity*, G.P. Putnam's Sons, New York, 1992.

Cameron, Julia, *The Artist's Way Everyday: A Year of Creative Living,* Jeremy P. Tarcher/Penguin, New York, 2009.

Cameron, Julia, *Prayers to the Great Creator: Prayers and Declarations for a Meaningful Life,* Tarcher/Perigee, New York, 2010.

Cameron, Julia, *The Right to Write,* Tarcher/Perigee, New York, 1999.

Cameron, Julia, *The Vein of Gold: A Journey to Your Creative Heart,* Jeremy P. Tarcher/Putnam, New York, 1996.

Campbell, Joseph, *The Power of Myth with Bob Moyers*, Anchor Publishers, New York, 2011.

Capacchione, Lucia, PhD., *The Power of Your Other Hand,* Conari Press, Newburyport, MA, 1988 and 2019.

carljungdepthpsychologysite.blog/2020/02/08/carl-jung-i-am-afraid-that-the-mere-fact-of-my-presence-takes-you-away-from-yourself/

Chödrön, Pema, *Getting Unstuck: Audio CD,* Sounds True, Inc., Louisville, CO, 2006.

Chödrön, Pema, *Start Where You Are: A Guide to Compassionate Living,* Shambhala Classics, Boston, MA, 1991.

Chödrön, Pema, *Taking the Leap: Freeing Ourselves from Old Habits and Fears*, Shambhala Publications, Inc., Boston, MA, 2009.

Chödrön, Pema, *Welcome the Unwelcome*, Shambhala Classics, Boston, MA, 2019.

Chödrön, Pema, *When Things Fall Apart: Heart Advice for Difficult Times*, Shambhala Classics, Boston, MA, 2000.

Coelho, Paulo, *The Alchemist*, Harper Collins, New York, 1988.

Coelho, Paulo, *Warrior of The Light*, Harper Collins, New York, 2003.

Coelho, Paulo, *Life: Selected Quotations*, Harper Collins Publishers, Slovakia, 2007.

Cole, Terri, *Boundary Boss: The Essential Guide to Talk True, Be Seen, and (Finally) Live Free*, Sounds True, Inc., Louisville, CO, 2021.

Comedians in Cars Getting Coffee. First Cup. "Michael Richard: It's Bubbly Time, Jerry." Directed by Jerry Seinfeld. 2012-2019 on Netflix. netflix.com/watch/80181892

Conny, Beth Mende, *Dare to Believe*, Peter Pauper Press, Inc., NY, 2000.

Csikszentmihalyi, Mihaly, *Flow: The Psychology of Optimal Experience*, HarperCollins, New York, 2008.

Day, Laura, *Practical Intuition*, Broadway Books, New York, 1997.

Day, Laura, *Welcome to Your Crisis*, Little, Brown & Company, New York, 2006.

Dyer, *Real Magic: Creating Miracles in Everyday Life*, HarperCollins, New York, 1992.

Dyer, Emerson, Irwin Edman, *Emerson's Essays*, Perennial Library, Harper & Row Publishers, New York/Thomas Y. Cromwell Company, 1926.

Einstein, Albert, *Bite-Size Einstein: Quotations on Just About Everything from the Greatest Mind of the Twentieth Century*, St. Martin's Press, New York, 2015.

Föllmi, Danielle and Olivier, *Awakenings: Asian Wisdom for Every Day,* Abrams Books, New York, NY 2006.

Fragakis, Allison, writingallison.com

Frankl, Viktor E., *Man's Search for Meaning*, Rider, London, 2004.

Gibran, Kahlil, *The Prophet*, Phone Media/Harper Collins Publishers, Sydney, Australia, 1923.

Gilbert, Elizabeth, *Big Magic: Creative Living Beyond Fear*, Riverhead Books, New York, 2015.

Gilbert, Elizabeth, *Your Elusive Creative Genius,* ted.com/talks/ elizabeth_gilbert_your_elusive_creative_genius, February 8, 2009.

goodreads.com

Hafiz, Ladinsky, Daniel, *The Gift: Poems by Hafiz*, Penguin Compass, New York, NY, 1999.

Hafiz, Ladinsky, Daniel, *I Heard God Laughing: Renderings of Hafiz*, Penguin Compass, New York, NY, 2006.

Hanh, Thich Nhat, *Peace Is Every Step: The Path of Mindfulness in Everyday Life,* Bantam Books, New York, 1991.

Hay, Louise, *You Can Heal Your Life,* Hay House, Carlsbad, CA, 1984.

Hay, Louise, Robert Holden, *Life Loves You: 7 Spiritual Practices to Heal Your Life*, Hay House, Carlsbad, CA, 2016.

Hayward, Susan, *A Guide for the Advanced Soul,* Devorss & Co., Camarillo, CA, 2010.

Hayward, Susan, *Begin It Now,* In-Tune Books, Avalon, Australia, 1987.

inspirationalstories.com

Jampolsky, Gerald G., *Love is Letting Go of Fear,* Ten Speed Press, Berkeley, CA, 2010.

Jokel, Robert, immunetocancer.com

Kennedy, Susan Ariel Rainbow Kennedy (SARK), *Make Your Creative Dreams Real: A Plan for Procrastinators, Perfectionists, Busy People, and People Who Would Really Rather Sleep All Day*, Atria Books, New York, 2005.

kidadl.com/articles/quotes-about-dance-to-help-you-feel-the-groove

Lamott, Anne, *Bird by Bird: Instructions on Writing and Life,* Anchor Publishing, New York, 1995.

Lamott, Anne, *Stitches*, Riverhead Books, New York, 2013.

libquotes.com

Linn, Denise, *Soul Coaching: 28 Days to Discover Your Authentic Self*, Hay House, Carlsbad, CA, 2011.

Kaufman, Barry, *Happiness Is a Choice*, Ballantine Books; New York, 1994.

Maria, Gwenievere, *In the Heart of God: A Journey Beyond Healing into the Sacred Realms of Creation*, AuthorHouse, 2005.

Martin Luther King, Jr., Nobel Lecture, www.nobelprize.org/prizes/peace/1964/king/lecture/ December 11, 1964.

Mohr, Tara Sophia, *Your Other Names: Poems by Tara Sophia Mohr*, Independent Publisher, California, 2011.

Motekaitis, Koren, *How She Really Does It Podcast,* howshereallydoesit.com

National Geographic Society, *Daily Calm: 365 Days of Serenity, Photos and Wisdom to Soothe Your Spirit*, National Geographic Society, Washington, D.C., 2013.

National Geographic Society, *Daily Kindness,: 365 Days of Compassion, Photos and Wisdom to Enrich Your Spirit*, National Geographic Society, Washington, D.C., 2017.

Nin, Anaïs, Herron, Paul, *The Quotable Anaïs Nin: 365 Quotations with Citations,* Sky Blue Press, 2014.

O'Donohue, John, Anam Cara, *A Book of Celtic Wisdom*, Harper Perennial, New York, 2004.

O'Sullivan, Noreen, *Look, Listen, Love: A Parent and Child's Guide to Emotional Freedom Tapping (EFT),* Lulu Press, Inc., Morrisville, NC, 2021.

Petras, Kathryn & Ross, *"It Always Seems Impossible Until It's Done,"* Workman Publishing Company, New York, 2014.

Pressman, Sarah D., Karen A. Matthews, PhD., Sheldon Cohen, PhD. Lynn M. Martire, PhD., Michael Scheier, PhD., Andrew Baum, PhD., and Richard Schulz, PhD., "Association of Enjoyable Leisure Activities with Psychological and Physical Well-being." *Psychosomatic Medicine: Journal of Biobehavioral Medicine*, volume 71, issue 7, pages 725-732., September 2009. ncbi.nlm.nih.gov/pmc/articles/PMC2863117/

psycom.net/epigenetics-trauma

quotehd.com

quotescover.com

quoteinvestigator.com

Roman, Sanaya, *Living With Joy: Keys to Spiritual Power and Personal Transformation*, HJKramer/New World Library, 2011.

Rosanoff, Nancy, *Intuition Workout: A Practical Guide to Discovering and Developing Your Inner Knowing,* Aslan Publishing, 1991.

SantoPietro, Nancy, *Feng Shui and Health*, Harmony Books, New York, 2002.

Schwartz, Richard, *No Bad Parts: Healing Trauma and Restoring Wholeness with the Internal Family Systems Model*, Sounds True, Boulder, CO, 2021.

Scott, Julie Jordan, www.CreativeLifeMidwife.com

Sherman, Donna, *Sparks In Action Podcast: Uplifting Each Other One Action at a Time,* Kingston, NY, 2021-2022.

Sherman, Donna, *Yoga Nidra with Donna Sherman: Total Relaxation Practices for Adults & Teens* (Amazon)

Siegel, Bernie, *Love, Medicine and Miracles,* HarperPerennial, NY, 1998.

Siegel, Bernie, *When You Realize How Perfect Everything Is*, Sacred Stories Publishing, 2020.

Siegel, Bernie, *No Endings, Only Beginnings: A Doctor's Notes on Living, Loving and Learning Who You Are*, Hay House, Carlsbad, California, 2020.

StaceySimpson.com (NLP, Reiki, and hypnotherapy)

Stark, Elizabeth, bookwritingworld.com

Stevenson, R. L., *Across the Plains*, Charles Scribner's Sons, New York, 1892.

Tagore, Rabindranath, *The Religion of Man*, Ravenio Books, 2015.

Tichio, Joe, *Greatest Inspirational Quotes,* San Bernardino, CA, 2014.

tinybuddha.com

Thoreau, Henry David, *Henry David Thoreau Collection*, Independent Publisher, 2021.

Tolkien, J.R.R., *The Fellowship of the Ring*, Del Rey/Penguin Random House, London, UK, 2012.

Tolkien, J.R.R., *The Hobbit,* Del Rey/Penguin Random House, London, 2012.

twildersociety.org/education/wilder-queries-exploring-quotations-1/

u1lib.org

un.org/depts/dhl/dag/time1953.htm

Vanzant, Iyanla, *Until Today: Daily Devotions for Spiritual Growth and Peace of Mind*, Simon & Schuster, 2000.

Wilde, Stuart, *Miracles*, Hay House, Carson, CA, 1983.

Wilde, Stuart, *Silent Power*, Hay House, Carson, CA 1983.

Williamson, Marianne, *A Return to Love*, HarperOne, New York, 1996.

Winfrey, Oprah, *O Magazine*, "What I Know for Sure" monthly columns, Hearst Magazines, New York 2000-2020.

Whitman, Walt, *Miracles* poem, poets.org/poem/miracles

Leaps of Gratitude

Thanks to My Circle

Writing a book like this one never happens in a vacuum. In fact, it has been the interchange of ideas, feedback, and support that has made the experience of this book's birthing process so rich for me personally.

I first want to thank my best friend, life partner for 31 years (and counting!), my husband Jim. Thank you for being there for me, especially during that week when the poems seemed to be falling from the sky. Those moments when you listened as I read my first poems to you, and when you supported me, and created space in our home so I could keep writing were so precious to me. Thank you for always being there with kind words of encouragement as this book, and my passion for this work has grown and taken form. You are my rock, my home, and my rudder as I keep sailing towards my dreams. One of those dreams is to continue supporting you in sailing towards yours. I love you so much.

I also want to thank our precious children Devin James and Kaya Grace. Thank you so much for supporting me, cheering me on, and being understanding as this book sometimes took on a life of its own, with papers and computers spread throughout our kitchen counter and home. You both delight and inspire me so much. I am constantly learning from you about what matters most, as well as how freeing it can be to simply create and live life just for the joy of it. You are continually showing me that more than anything, life is about loving, enjoying, appreciating, and creating beauty. May you both always follow your hearts and remember that you have magical gifts to offer the world just by being you, and how very loved you are. Your dad and I love you both so very much.

This book would not be what it is without the incredibly inspiring, heartfelt, open, creative energy of all those who have participated in my free 28-Day Flow Challenges. I am so grateful to you all, and have been continually inspired by your courage, sharing, insights, ideas, openness, intuition, and commitment to following your true inner voices. Each time I lead a Flow Challenge, I am constantly wowed by your creativity and wisdom, as well as by how life's miraculous synchronicities connect us, often at the perfect time. You have each taught me so much, and I am so grateful to you for continuing to show up, month after month, answering the call to flow, being there by my side, and trusting me with your insights and life stories. It has been an absolute honor, and I look forward to our circle continuing to expand, and more epiphanies ahead!

I also want to thank my mother Barbara, who is always up for an adventure, has always been so supportive of my creativity, is so artistic and creative herself, and has such a loving heart. It has been such an honor to have you participating in my Flow Challenges from the beginning. Your commitment to the expansion of your spirit and offering an empathetic, peaceful energy to the world continually inspire me. Thank you also for reading an early version of this manuscript and supporting my writing and my dreams. I love you!

I have been blessed to be part of a small, sweet circle of writers who have supported me in my writing dreams and have become like soul sisters to me during the two years in which this book took form. Thank you, Arleen Smith, Cheryl Lauer, Malikah Wright, and Dorette Adams for cheering me on as I've written and edited this book, as well as providing editorial feedback along the way. Arleen, your quick overnight read of my manuscript with insightful comments was such an incredible gift and so affirming. You are so brilliant and have such a generous spirit. Thank you!

I have also been blessed to have two very talented editors in my life who have been supporting my flow challenges, connecting me with other creative souls, and who have provided instrumental direction as the final version of this book unfolded. First, a big thanks my beloved sister Kimberly Smith who patiently read so many versions of this book, offering such rich insights and ideas each time. I have been so touched by your intellect, editing talents, depth, presence, wisdom, and support of my work, as well as your willingness to show up full-on when I've needed you most. The other is Carrie Machleder. Carrie, your patience, honesty, gentle direction, friendship, creativity, insights, and editing gifts helped this book become what it is today. You are truly an artist. Thank you.

I am also blessed to be supported by a larger circle of friends, fellow creators, and family members who have provided the role of readers, reviewers, proofreaders, sounding boards, and who have engaged in lively conversations with me about flow and creativity, as well as offered strong support and encouragement that is reflected in the pages of this book. While in no way all-inclusive, I am deeply grateful to my dear creative friends including Ron and Pam Brandsdorfer, Laura Briggs, Jill Cifelli, June Cook, Lyenochka Djakov, Jacqueline Genovesi, Katie Grant, Liza Marasa, Katie McKee, Loren Medwick, Noreen O'Sullivan, Maureen Smith, and my larger extended family and in-laws as well as my brothers Scott Smith and Hugh Smith for your support and encouragement. Thank you!

I am also deeply grateful to all the teachers, fellow writers, and creators who have been part of my journey, many of whom are referenced in the resources section of this book. Even if it has been many years since our paths have crossed, I am very grateful to you for shining your light in the world and encouraging me to share my gifts.

Lastly, I also want to thank Sue Lilledahl. You have acted as a creative midwife, not just in this book's unfolding, but in supporting me in reclaiming my calling as a writer. You have taught me to work with rather than against my own unique creative processes and natural ways of being. You truly understand the emotional side of the creative process, and the truth behind artistic highs and lows. You have held the space for me to see my own light and what is possible from a bright perspective. I will always be grateful to you for your ability to truly see, accept, and understand me, your role in helping me to truly see, know, and accept myself, and most of all, your encouragement to keep writing. Off to writing my next book! Thank you.

I dedicate this book to the memory of my father Hugh with deep gratitude. While he's been gone for many years now, I feel closer to him with each passing day. Thank you, Dad, for loving me so much, encouraging my writing, and always being there when I've needed you.

About the Author

Laurie E. Smith is an intuitive and creativity coach, inspirational writer, and workshop facilitator. She loves writing as much as she absolutely can, sharing her heart and creative work even when it's imperfect, and supporting others who are on similar journeys. She lives with her husband and two kids in the San Francisco Bay area. You can learn more about her work at www.LaurieSmith.com.

Join Laurie's Circle of Creative Friends

You are invited to sign up for my free 28-day Flow Challenges and weekly email newsletter at:

www.LaurieSmith.com

All are welcome! My website also includes my current offerings and information about flow.

I would love to hear how you are using the material in this book in your own life, any insights you've gained on your own creative journey, or feedback you'd like to share. Thanks!

You can email me directly at:
Laurie@LaurieSmith.com

You can also reach me at this email address for requests about interviews, group workshops, collaborations, reprints, or bulk orders.

Here's where you can find me on social media:

Instagram - @LaurieSmith_inspired

LinkedIn - @LaurieSmith-inspired

Free Facebook Group:
Circle of Creative Friends
facebook.com/groups/28dayflowchallenge

Thanks for leaping with me!

CPSIA information can be obtained
at www.ICGtesting.com
Printed in the USA
BVHW020018140223
658390BV00009B/321